Sludge

Sludge

What Stops Us from Getting Things Done and
What to Do about It

Cass R. Sunstein

The MIT Press

Cambridge, Massachusetts | London, England

This book was set in Stone Serif and Stone Sans by Westchester Publishing Services. Printed and bound in the United States of America.

Library of Congress Cataloging-in-Publication Data

Names: Sunstein, Cass R., author.
Title: Sludge : what stops us from getting things done and what to do about it / Cass R. Sunstein.
Description: Cambridge, Massachusetts : The MIT Press, 2021. | Includes bibliographical references and index.
Identifiers: LCCN 2020033683 | ISBN 9780262045780 (hardcover)
Subjects: LCSH: Bureaucracy--United States. | Administrative procedure--United States. | Government paperwork--United States. | Paperwork (Office practice)--United States.
Classification: LCC JK421 .S885 2021 | DDC 302.3/50973--dc23
LC record available at https://lccn.loc.gov/2020033683

10   9   8   7   6   5   4   3   2   1

Sludge. noun. Thick, soft, wet mud or a similar viscous mixture of liquid and solid components, especially the product of an industrial or refining process.

—Oxford Online Dictionary, 2019

Contents

Preface

This book is a product of a failure. During the presidency of Barack Obama, I was privileged to serve as the administrator of the White House Office of Information and Regulatory Affairs—OIRA, as it is called. OIRA is an obscure office, with a small staff of about fifty people, but it plays a significant role in the US government. It helps oversee the operation of the regulatory state, including health care, environmental protection, civil rights, highway safety, occupational health, food safety, agriculture, even homeland security. But it was originally created by the Paperwork Reduction Act (PRA), enacted in 1980, and one of its central missions is, well, to reduce paperwork.

Which brings me to the failure. For most of my time at OIRA, I was focused on large and dramatic issues: economic growth, health care reform, financial stability, climate change, clean air, clean water, race and sex discrimination, public health, highway safety. Paperwork reduction mattered, for sure, but it was not the highest priority. That wasn't exactly wrong, but it wasn't quite

right, either. Countless programs, potentially benefiting so many people, end up failing because of excessive
paperwork. Sometimes administrative burdens reduce
economic growth and produce widespread unfairness.
They even make people sick.

Sometimes the victims are businesses: from the largest to the smallest, from the well-established to start-
ups. Sometimes the victims are people who need some
kind of license or permit, perhaps to work. Sometimes
the victims are the most vulnerable members of society: people who are in poor health, disabled, depressed,
elderly, or poor. Sometimes paperwork and associated
burdens hammer identifiable groups, including women
and people of color. It was not until relatively late in my
four-year stint that my team and I began to go hard at
the problem. It was too late, and it was too little.

In the years since that time, we have learned an
immense amount about the damage done by paperwork
requirements, waiting time, reporting requirements,
clearance processes, and the like. Some of what we
have learned involves what is actually happening on the
ground—what public officials are doing to people, and
how they are harming them, by making them jump
through an assortment of hoops. Some of what we have
learned involves the human mind and its limits, which
help to explain why such burdens can be so devastat-
ing. Some of what we have learned involves the private
sector, which can damage its customers, and its own
employees, by imposing sludge.

In many cases, officials themselves have no clue about the consequences of paperwork and related requirements. In many other cases, they know exactly what they are doing. That is true of hospitals, businesses, universities, and other institutions as well.

When people are required to jump through hoops, all sorts of bad things might happen, some of them surprising. One of the least surprising is that many people stop jumping. That might be a reasonable thing to do or essential to people's self-preservation, but in many cases it is also a kind of tragedy. The good news is that a lot can be done to help.

A roadmap of what is to come: Chapter 1 clarifies the key concepts and offers a short account of the underlying problem. Chapter 2 investigates why sludge is so harmful, with special reference to behavioral science. It emphasizes the problems of inertia, present bias, and scarcity (cognitive, not economic). In combination, these are a potent brew. They help account for the damage done by sludge—much more, often, than anyone ever intended.

Chapter 3 explains that sludge is a product of architecture. Sometimes deliberately, sometimes by accident, it has a major effect on outcomes. It could easily be otherwise. Chapter 4 offers a brisk, illustrative tour of the not-wonderful world of sludge, with reference to benefit programs, occupational licensing, student visas, and constitutional rights. Different people, with different values, will have different reactions to the level of burdens in different areas—but with respect to sludge, there is a great deal of room for people who disagree on fundamental issues to make common cause.

Chapter 5 investigates the legitimate reasons for sludge—above all, *program integrity*, which means that sludge can be a way to ensure that people who apply for things actually deserve to get them. People should not receive money to which they are not entitled, and sludge helps to prevent unjustified receipts. Record-keeping can also be important; public and private institutions impose sludge to ensure that they can learn how programs are doing. In addition, sludge can be a way of preventing recklessness and impulsiveness; it can increase the likelihood that people really want to do what they are about to do. By emphasizing justifications for sludge, chapter 5 can be seen as an effort to restore the balance.

Chapter 6 elaborates the idea of Sludge Audits, and urges that they are likely to pay large dividends. The government should be conducting many of them. The same is true of private institutions, which could save a lot of money and a lot of time and improve well-being for countless people (including their own employees). Chapter 6 also explores potential legal reforms, coming from all branches of government. While my focus here is on the United States, my hope is that these reforms can be adopted in many nations.

Chapter 7 is a brief manifesto, identifying the most precious thing that human beings are blessed to have.

1
A Curse

In all likelihood, your life has been made worse because of sludge—a "viscous mixture," consisting of frictions that prevent you from doing what you want to do or from going where you want to go.[1] My first goal here is to understand why sludge is so harmful. My second goal is to see what might be done to reduce that harm.

Sludge comes from private and public institutions. It comes from small companies and from large ones. It comes from national governments and from state and local authorities. It comes from the United Nations, the European Commission, and the World Bank. Lawyers impose sludge. So do courts. So do doctors and hospitals. Banks certainly impose sludge. Although the problem of sludge is worse in some countries than in others, it can be found in every nation on the planet. And while my focus is on the United States, the basic lessons are much broader. Sludge is built into the human condition, and we need to start to remove it, piece by piece.

In many cases, sludge imposes economic harm. In other cases, it damages public health. In the worst cases, it kills. Every day, it impairs education; often it deprives people of educational opportunity. It cripples economic growth. It decreases employment and stifles entrepreneurship and innovation. It hurts patients, parents, teachers, doctors, nurses, employees, customers, investors, and developers. It compromises fundamental rights, including the right to vote and the right to be free from discrimination on the basis of race and sex. It is a pervasive source of inequality.

Sludge can also be an assault on human dignity. Confronting sludge, and having to find a way to overcome it, can create a sense of humiliation. Kafka captures that; his novels depict a world in which people cannot navigate life or escape their predicament because of that viscous mixture. If sludge stops you from voting or from getting some kind of license, you might feel as if you do not count. People without much money struggle with sludge. It hurts all of us, but if you are sick, old, disabled, or poor, or if you don't have a lot of education, sludge is a curse.

In 2020, the city of West Sacramento, California, took a small step toward breaking the curse. It automatically admitted every high school student in the area to college (and also offered a scholarship award of $200).[2] As Mayor Christopher Cabandon put it, "Imagine no one in your family has ever gone to college and you open up an envelope with a letter of admission and a scholarship award." He added that the new effort "will make it just as simple to go from high school to college as it is to go from kindergarten to first grade."

As we shall see, the idea of automatic admission grows directly out of behavioral science. Even a little sludge, in the form of an application process, can have large effects. There is every reason to think that taking away the sludge will help a lot of high schoolers to end up in college. More officials should be doing that.

Sludge is everywhere in our lives. For a glimpse, consider the following cases:

1. Poor students are entitled to financial aid for college. To obtain that aid, they have to fill out a form. It has dozens of questions, and many students find it challenging to answer some of them. As a result, they decide not to apply for aid at all.

2. To obtain benefits under a health care law, people must navigate a complicated website. A lot of them do not understand the questions that they are being asked. For many people, the application takes a long time. Some of them give up.

3. To register a complaint about defective products, consumers are required to go through a time-consuming process. The necessary forms call for detailed information about where the product was originally purchased and how it was used. Some consumers do not have easy access to that information. Others fear that their privacy might be invaded. Many of them decide not to fill out the forms at all.

4. To vote, many citizens of Georgia have to wait in a long line. Sometimes the wait takes four hours or more.

A number of people cannot spare that time. A number of others think that it is too unpleasant. Some of them do not go to the polls at all. Others leave after an hour.

5. A cell phone company markets some of its products with mail-in rebates. On some products, consumers are entitled to a rebate of $200. The company is well aware that many consumers will be excited about the potential rebate—but they fail to mail in the forms.

6. To fix a broken laptop, consumers have to make a telephone call to a customer service representative and then make an appointment. Once they arrive at the relevant stores, waiting times are often long; they can be up to two hours.

7. A professor is asked to review an academic article for a journal. To do so, she must register at the journal's website. Registration is confusing and complicated. As a result, she declines to review the article.

Some of these cases are trivial; others are not. All of them involve sludge, and if you have ever tried to get a license from public officials or some kind of permit, you have encountered it. (To get a driver's license, you have to get through sludge. Sometimes there's only a little of it; sometimes there's a lot.) But what, exactly, does the term encompass?

If sludge is understood to consist of frictions that separate people from what they want to get, the concept is not entirely mysterious. Much sludge involves waiting time (in person, on the phone, even online).

Much of it involves reporting burdens (as when people are required to fill out weekly reports, explaining what they have been doing with their lives). Much of it consists of dreary or duplicative application requirements, including time spent online, which might be required if people are seeking to obtain money, medical care, a job, a visa, a permit, or some kind of life-saving help. Much of it involves travel (as when people need to show up somewhere for an in-person interview).

Much sludge involves confusing administrative burdens—requiring people to obtain information, to figure out whom to call, to find out exactly what they are supposed to do. Much of it involves clearance processes, familiar within government (as when ten people must "sign off" on some document or initiative) and also in the private sector (as at private universities and hospitals). Training requirements—imposed, for example, on doctors, nurses, pilots, truck drivers, and flight attendants— count as sludge, though they may of course be justified.

Sludge includes, but goes beyond, "red tape" (itself a vague idea). If you have to wait in line to vote, or if you have to go to a government office for an interview before receiving a license, you are not exactly facing red tape. But you have to deal with sludge. Sludge is not bureaucracy, though it overlaps with it. The Department of Energy is a bureaucracy, but it is not sludge (though it imposes plenty of it).

Sludge can be seen as a kind of *transaction cost*, a familiar term in economics. But the house of transaction costs has many rooms, and some transaction costs are not sludge. For example, legal fees and brokerage fees are often characterized as transaction costs; they do not count as sludge. The important idea of *admin*, developed by Elizabeth Emens,[3] includes sludge, but a lot of admin (such as household labor) is not sludge.

Still, the term is not hard-edged, and it does leave unresolved questions. I think it is best not to fuss much over that problem. It is challenging to produce necessary and sufficient conditions for sludge, but in context, it is usually clear enough whether or not we are dealing with it.[4] For conceptual clarity, we should not include strictly monetary incentives or disincentives. Suppose that consumers are told that they must pay a specified amount to obtain insurance, that they have to pay an application fee to enroll in a health care program, or that they can obtain a better seat on an airplane for a small additional amount. In such cases, they are unlikely to be thrilled, but they are not facing sludge. A ban is not sludge; if people are forbidden to smoke in public places, sludge is not the problem.

A mandate may or may not be sludge, depending on what, exactly, is being mandated. Is sludge itself being mandated? If people are told that they must obtain health insurance, they are facing sludge to the extent that the process of obtaining health insurance involves friction (such as significant paperwork requirements). If people are told that they have to go through an unnecessarily complex process to get a doctor's help with depression or anxiety, they are certainly being required to wade through sludge. If people learn that they need to fill out a lengthy form and have an interview to participate in the Global Entry program (a terrific program in the United States, making travel far less sludgy), they have to face sludge: a little sludge now, in return for a lot less sludge in the future.

Not long ago, I asked a group of students about the health care they received at a large university. My question: What could be improved? Two of them singled out the problem of mental health. They said that in order to make an appointment for a mental health issue, they had to make two separate phone calls and fill out some complicated paperwork. They added that the problem of mental illness is stigmatized and that when you are suffering, the last thing you want to do is to find your way through sludge.

One of them reported that after a little frustration, she decided that it just wasn't worthwhile to try to make an appointment. This story does not have a tragic ending, but all over the world, people with mental health problems have to deal with sludge. Many of them give up.

Is sludge always bad? Certainly not. Sludge can be excessive, insufficient, or optimal. If you are going to do something major with your life—say, get divorced—sludge might be an excellent idea. (We will get to the details in due course.) "Are you sure you want to . . . ?" questions online can be annoying, but they provide both individual and social benefits. If people are asked to say whether they are sure that they want to delete some important file, waive their legal rights, send an angry email, or post something on social media, the resulting burdens might be an effort to prevent mistakes or reck-lessness. In due course, I shall provide a detailed account of the legitimate reasons for sludge. But I am here mostly to bury sludge, not to praise it.

Nudge and Sludge

At this point, some people might wondering about the relationship between sludge and nudge. For orientation: nudges are private or public initiatives that steer people in particular directions but that also allow them to go their own way. A reminder is a nudge; so is a warning. A GPS device nudges; a default rule, automatically enroll-ing people in some program, is a nudge. To qualify as a nudge, an initiative must not impose significant mate-rial incentives (including disincentives). Those who like nudging often emphasize the importance of "making it easy." If the goal is to change behavior, it always makes sense to ask: Why aren't people doing it anyway? Once we obtain the answer, we can take steps to remove the obstacle—which might be sludge.

It should be clear that nudging can be used for both good and bad purposes. Consumers might be defaulted into an expensive health care plan that fails to suit their needs. Consumers might be defaulted into an insur-ance plan, for cell phones or laptops, that is not at all in their interests. Consumers might be nudged, through behaviorally informed advertisements, into buying cigarettes or alcohol, even if doing so makes their lives go worse. Nudging is a tool, no less than subsidies, fines, and criminal prohibitions. To evaluate nudges, we need to know their welfare effects—what they are achieving and at what cost. The best test is simple: Are nudges increasing people's welfare? Are they improving people's lives? Of course, it is true that the idea of welfare needs to be specified, and it is important to emphasize that many people emphasize the importance of fair distribution and would want to pay particular attention to the welfare of the most disadvantaged members of society (*prioritarianism*).[5]

Efforts to ensure that people do not act recklessly can be characterized either as (helpful) nudges or as sludge. Such efforts are designed to help people act more deliberatively rather than impulsively. The vivid title of an important article makes the point: "Handgun Waiting Periods Reduce Gun Deaths."[6] In this light, we can see that some helpful nudges reduce frictions ("make it easy"), while other helpful nudges increase frictions ("make it hard"). Nudges that increase frictions can be seen as *deliberation-promoting*, in the sense that they have the goal of encouraging people to think carefully and to give certain courses of action (a purchase, a change in a health care or payment plan, a major move of some kind) a kind of sober second thought. In the context of consumer behavior, deliberation-promoting nudges can be a blessing; they are an important way of nudging, and in many settings, there should be more of them.

We can therefore construct a table with four cells (see table 1.1). Nudge and sludge overlap in cell (2). Though I will have a fair bit to say about that cell, the principal concern here is cell (4). Reasonable people can, of course, debate its precise content. Obstacles to navigability—as through complex sites, multiple questions, confusing words and phrases, manipulative terms—are certainly forms of sludge.

A War on Sludge

As part of the response to the coronavirus pandemic of 2020, the United States waged a war on sludge. Most people didn't notice, but it happened.

Table 1.1

	Low friction	High friction
Good	Helpful "make it easy" nudge (e.g., simplification, airport maps, automatic enrollment in good pension plan) (1)	Deliberating-promoting nudge or sludge (e.g., "Are you sure you want to . . . ?"; cooling off periods; waiting periods) (2)
Bad	Harmful "make it easy" nudge (e.g., automatic enrollment in some costly, worthless program) (3)	Sludge (e.g., form-filling nightmares; long waiting times for drivers' licenses or visas) (4)

In a short period, public officials took a series of aggressive steps to reduce administrative barriers that had been imposed on doctors, nurses, hospitals, patients, and beneficiaries of essential public and private services. With respect to sludge, the pandemic concentrated the bureaucratic mind, leading to impressive and brisk reforms. A few examples:

- Under the Supplemental Nutrition Assistance Program (formerly known as the Food Stamps Program), would-be beneficiaries have long had to complete in-person interviews before they are approved for benefits. The US Department of Agriculture (USDA) waived that requirement. It gave states "blanket approval" to give out benefits to people who are entitled to them.[7]

- The Internal Revenue Service originally announced that in order to qualify for payments under the Families First Coronavirus Response Act, people would have to file tax returns—even if they are Social Security recipients who typically do not do that. The sludge would have meant that many people would never get money to which they are legally entitled. Under public pressure, and probably seeing the foolishness of the idea, the Department of Treasury reversed course—and said that Social Security recipients would receive the money automatically.

- Some of the most aggressive sludge-reduction efforts came from the Department of Health and Human

Services.[8] Many paperwork, reporting, and auditing requirements were eliminated. Importantly, dozens of medical services were authorized through tele-health. In the agency's own words, the government "is allowing telehealth to fulfill many face-to-face visit requirements for clinicians to see their patients in inpatient rehabilitation facilities, hospice and home health." In addition, the government allowed Medicare to be used to pay laboratory technicians to travel to people's homes to collect specimens for testing—thus eliminating the need for people to travel to healthcare facilities for tests (and risk getting sick).

- The Food and Drug Administration (FDA) granted states much greater flexibility in multiple domains. For example, it permitted the New York State Department of Health to allow patient testing in circumstances in which formal authorization by the FDA (and accompanying sludge) would previously have been required.[9]

Why did all this happen? One reason for the pandemic-induced war on sludge was a new cost-benefit calculus: when countless people are getting sick or poor, the harmful effects of paperwork and other burdens grow exponentially. In normal times, it might be acceptable or sensible to tolerate a delay and to require people to do some less-than-fun work in order to ensure that they really do qualify for benefits, or to protect against some kind of social harm. But if people are at risk of dying, we should be willing to accept less-than-perfect accuracy or less-than-ideal safeguards. That might be the price for saving lives.

The more general point is that when public officials (or others) impose sludge, they are making some kind of judgment about whether doing so is a good idea. Sometimes the judgment is intuitive and relatively informal; it is not preceded by numbers. It might be based on a belief that if people are to obtain certain benefits, the least they can do is to show up for an interview to prove that they qualify. Sometimes the judgment is rooted in evidence, offering a basis for deciding how much sludge to impose. But when new circumstances arise, it might become clear that the current amount of sludge is not the right amount of sludge. The harms imposed by sludge are often invisible. In the context of a pandemic, they are there for all to see.

Another reason is subtler and more fundamental. In the midst of the coronavirus pandemic, countless people were scared, confused, overwhelmed, or anxious about their health or their finances. They might have been dealing with young children at home, with sick or elderly friends and relatives, or with both. They might have been sick themselves. Because they were frightened and preoccupied, they did not have a lot of mental bandwidth to manage sludge, whether it came from the government or the private sector. Sludge could defeat them. And it could do so with respect to programs on which their economic situation, or their health, depended.

For many people, that is true in the best of times, of course—which is one reason that every year is a good year for a war on sludge.[10] One of the worst features of a sludge-pervaded city, state, or nation is that people become inured to it; their preferences adapt to what surrounds them, and they may not even complain much about it.[11] It is part of life's furniture. But during a pandemic, the stakes grow dramatically, and the bandwidth problem has become immeasurably worse for many millions of people. The furniture has to be moved. If the goal is to get medical help to people or help them survive economically, simplification, waivers, and automaticity are good watchwords. Sludge removal might not seem like the highest priority, but it can make the difference between relative comfort and acute hardship, or even life and death.

Faster

Providing people with help during a pandemic is especially urgent, of course, but the benefits of reducing sludge can be found in countless domains. For a quick understanding of those benefits, consider the TSA PreCheck program, designed to speed up security lines at airports. The program, adopted by the United States in 2011, was created on the theory that the standard security processes impose excessive sludge on many travelers. Those enrolled in the program are able to take advantage of expedited screening and shorter lines—a clear effort at sludge reduction. In a recent year, five million people were enrolled. What are its benefits?

Let us assume, conservatively, that on average, those five million people use the program four times per year. (I am bracketing the disruption caused by the COVID-19 pandemic.) If so, we are speaking of twenty million uses. Let us also assume, plausibly, that on average, a user of the program saves twenty minutes per trip. If so, we are speaking of four hundred million hours saved per year. Let us assume, finally, that an hour is worth, on average, twenty-seven dollars.[12] If so, the benefit of the TSA program is $1.08 billion per year. In any year, few regulations generate benefits of that magnitude. To be sure, we do not know the costs of the program, but it would be astonishing if they came anywhere near $1.08 billion.

True, most sludge-reduction efforts are unlikely to have benefits in excess of $1 billion. But if a specified amount of time is saved by a large population of consumers—say, one hundred thousand—the benefits will not exactly be trivial. Importantly, monetizing time savings is hardly sufficient to capture those benefits. Some of the benefits are psychological: a reduction of frustration, anxiety, and perhaps a sense of humiliation. If sludge is reduced, a sense of dignity and respect is restored. A society pervaded by sludge humiliates people, and sludge reduction removes the humiliation. (I will return to this point.)

But time savings are only part of the picture, and the same is true of psychological benefits. We have seen enough to know that sludge-reduction efforts can greatly improve access to goods and services, including money, health care, valuable products, education, job training, and economic opportunities. For ordinary people, sludge reduction can change lives. For companies, they can increase sales and goodwill. For employees, they can significantly increase well-being. For governments, they can greatly improve performance.

The United States has long had a program that gives free school meals (breakfast and lunch) to poor children. For many years, the problem was that many parents did not enroll their kids. It is not clear why. Perhaps they were too busy. Perhaps they did not understand what they were supposed to do. Perhaps a communication from the government frightened or confused them. In response to persistently low take-up rates, Congress allowed the USDA to adopt a direct certification program, which means that parents do not have to take the trouble to enroll their children at all.[13] If states or local educational agencies have enough information to know that children are eligible, they are automatically enrolled. In recent years, more than fifteen million children benefited from the program and others like it (about 91 percent of the eligible population).[14] Sludge removal has had a large impact on the lives of those children and their families.

In the same vein, simplification of the Free Application for Financial Student Aid (FAFSA) dramatically increases the likelihood that low-income people will apply for aid and eventually enroll in college.[15] Merely by simplifying the form, officials can give people without a lot of money—including numerous people of color—a chance to attend college. A number of states have adopted automatic voter registration, which means that if eligible citizens interact with a state agency (say, by receiving a driver's license), they are registered as voters.[16] In less than a year, Oregon's automatic registration program produced more than 250,000 new voters, and almost one hundred thousand of them actually voted.[17] Outside of the United States, automatic voter registration is not uncommon. And the private sector can do immeasurably more to reduce sludge—to help workers choose among healthcare plans, to make life easier for consumers and employees with ideas or complaints, and to help people to avoid serious risks.[18]

11.4 Billion Hours

Enacted in 1979, the Paperwork Reduction Act[19] was meant as a deregulatory statute. It was designed to minimize the paperwork burden imposed on the American people and to maximize the benefit of the information obtained. In that way, it was meant to reduce sludge. Its key provision[20] states:

> With respect to the collection of information and the control of paperwork, the Director [of the Office of Management and Budget] shall—
>
> (1) review and approve proposed agency collections of information;
>
> (2) coordinate the review of the collection of information associated with Federal procurement and acquisition by the Office of Information and Regulatory Affairs with the Office of Federal Procurement Policy, with particular emphasis on applying information technology to improve the efficiency and effectiveness of Federal procurement, acquisition and payment, and to reduce information collection burdens on the public;
>
> (3) *minimize the Federal information collection burden, with particular emphasis on those individuals and entities most adversely affected;*
>
> (4) *maximize the practical utility of and public benefit from information collected by or for the Federal Government;*
>
> (5) establish and oversee standards and guidelines by which agencies are to estimate the burden to comply with a proposed collection of information.

For present purposes, the most important provisions are the italicized (3) and (4). The word *minimize* suggests that paperwork burdens should be no greater than necessary to promote the agency's goals. The central idea seems to be one of *cost-effectiveness*: of two approaches to promoting those goals, the least burdensome must be chosen.

Taking the word *minimize* together with the phrase *maximize the practical utility and public benefit*, we can also understand the PRA to suggest a kind of cost-benefit test: *The benefits of paperwork burdens must justify their costs.* And yet there is no systematic effort, to date, to see which burdens pass that test. Nor is there an opportunity for people to challenge paperwork burdens in court—for example, to get them struck down, in the standard legal parlance, as "arbitrary" or "capricious."

All this creates serious problems. Many people like deregulation, seeing it as a way of freeing up the economy from pointless restrictions. Many people deplore it, seeing it as a way of eliminating essential safeguards of health and safety. Love it or hate it, it is generally taken to refer to the elimination of the kinds of burdens imposed through regulations that order people to do specific things: reduce air pollution, increase the minimum wage, make cars safer, put graphic warning labels on cigarettes, decrease cancer risks to workers.

Elimination of sludge is not always included in the category of deregulation.[21] It should be. In view of the costs of sludge, material and otherwise, sludge reduction should be a high priority—and it should be able to produce enthusiasm, even a burst of applause, from people who disagree about a great deal else. Whenever the government imposes paperwork burdens, it ought to ask a cost-benefit question. Are those burdens really justified? How much do they help? How much do they hurt? The government should also ask distributional questions: Who, exactly, is being helped, and who is being hurt? Is sludge hurting the most vulnerable members of society?

Is sludge being imposed on people who are poor or desperate, or in some sense struggling?

The PRA requires the Office of Management and Budget to produce an annual report, called the Information Collection Budget (ICB) of the US government.[22] The ICB quantifies the annual paperwork burden that the US government imposes on its citizens. The 2017 report found that Americans spent 11.4 billion hours on federal paperwork.[23] The number has been growing over time.

It is worth pausing over that 11.4-billion-hour figure. Suppose that we assembled every resident of Chicago, and insisted that for the entirety of a year, each one must work forty hours a week, engaged in just one task: filling out federal forms. By the end of the year, the 2.7 million Chicagoans will not have come anywhere close to the annual paperwork burden placed on Americans.

The 11.4 billion hours take a significant toll.[24] If we value an hour of work at twenty-seven dollars,[25] we are speaking of the equivalent of $307.8 billion—more than quadruple the budget of the Department of Education, about six times the budget of the Department of State, and about ten times the budget of the Department of Energy. We have seen enough to know that the monetary figures greatly understate the problem. Sludge can make it difficult or impossible for people to avoid crushing hardship.

What are we going to do about that?

2
Sludge Hurts

If you have to stand in line for hours to vote, you might not vote. If you have to get official permission to practice your religion, you might not practice your religion. It's one thing to say that if the government takes your property, it has to pay you just compensation. But what do you have to do to get that compensation? The Constitution might give you a right to a fair trial. But if you have been accused of a crime, how, exactly, do you go about getting that?

Much of the law of freedom of speech is about sludge; it renders certain kinds of sludge unconstitutional. Under US law, there is something close to a flat ban on "prior restraints," defined as restrictions on speech *before* people are allowed to say what they want. If you have to get a license before you can protest on public streets, you might not engage in protests.[1] Constitutional law is alert to that point, and judges strike down licensing schemes for speech. The ban on prior restraints is a ban on sludge.[2] Authoritarian leaders, determined to squelch rights, impose a lot of sludge. That is how they start, and it might get them most of what they want.

Eliminating sludge transforms people into rightsholders, as opposed to supplicants. Creating sludge does just the opposite.

A Small Example

Quite apart from the coronavirus pandemic, the sludge imposed on doctors and patients can literally kill.[3] Efforts to reduce sludge in the domain of health care, through private initiative and through law, save lives.[4] As a vivid example, consider the case of opioid use. Suboxone has become the linchpin of medication for opioid use disorder (OUD), and it is now considered the gold standard for treating that disorder. Suboxone combines buprenorphine and naloxone. It reduces cravings and makes overdoses, even fatal ones, far less likely.

For treating OUD, emergency rooms present an important opportunity. When patients overdose or just want help, they are treated and stabilized, but long-term Suboxone regimens are not routinely commenced. This lifesaving approach should be the standard of care, but it has not yet become so. Why is this? The answer is sludge.[5]

By federal law, physicians in the United States must obtain a special *X waiver* in order to prescribe buprenorphine, one of the active ingredients in Suboxone. (Yes, the name really is X waiver.) The required time and administrative burdens required to obtain the X waiver have discouraged many otherwise willing physicians from becoming able to prescribe it. If more physicians obtained X waivers and offered Suboxone to motivated patients known to be at high risk of relapse, fewer people would die.

The sludge involved in getting an X waiver has defeated many willing physicians. A lot of them pay and sign up for training sessions, but they do not finish the combined eight-hour modules. Even among those who go to that trouble and pay the fee, some 30 percent fail to complete required post-training forms. It is true, of course, that some people insist that the training is important. But the question is whether, in its current form, its benefits justify its costs.

In an effort to overcome sludge, many physicians are aggressively encouraging their colleagues to "get waivered." That's good, but a far better policy would be to remove the X waiver requirement entirely. The effect of removing that requirement would be substantial. It would make the pathway for OUD prescription smoother for a great number of physicians who want to do the right thing. It would prevent unnecessary deaths.

This is just one example. Every day, nurses and doctors must deal with unnecessary and mind-numbing sludge that costs a great deal of time and money and that ultimately reduces the quality of care. The large costs of health care in the United States are produced, in significant part, by sludge, which means that reducing it would

dramatically cut those costs and bring significant benefits to hospitals, doctors, nurses, and patients alike.[6]

Diverse Costs

It should now be clear that sludge imposes different kinds
of costs. Some of them are easy to monetize; others are
not. From one point of view, of course, there is no important distinction between the two. After all, time can be
monetized—perhaps to the tune of twenty-seven dollars
per hour (as discussed in chapter 1). But for time, any
unitary number is too crude. For a lot of people, an hour is
worth less than that; for a lot of people, it is worth much
more. A great deal will depend on what people are asked
to *do* with that time. For some people, an hour dealing
with an in-person interview to obtain important benefits
is very painful—and they would give up a fair amount
not to have to do it. Other people don't so much mind
that.

If the costs of sludge are emotional (involving, for
example, frustration and humiliation), it will be especially challenging to develop monetary equivalents, but
perhaps we could do that as well. If we believe that all
costs are the same, then sludge might simply be characterized as a kind of cost, whose magnitude can, in principle,
be turned into monetary equivalents. But qualitative dis-
tinctions are useful, even essential. There is an important
qualitative distinction between (say) a tax or a fine on

the one hand and an endless and mind-numbing form-filling requirement on the other. There is an important qualitative distinction between having to pay a small license fee and being asked a series of embarrassing and intrusive personal questions as a condition for receiving a license or a visa. Some kinds of sludge make people feel like second-class citizens.

Why Sludge Matters

To understand why sludge matters, let's begin with the assumption that people are fully rational and that in deciding whether to wade through sludge, they make some calculation about costs and benefits. Even if the benefits of that wading are high, the costs might prove overwhelming.[7] Those costs might involve acquisition of *information*, which might be difficult and expensive. They might involve *time*, which people might not have. They might be *psychological*, in the sense that they involve frustration, stigma, and humiliation. For any of those reasons, it might be very difficult to navigate or overcome the sludge.

In some cases, getting through sludge might be literally impossible; for example, it simply may not be feasible for people to fill out the necessary forms. They may not have and may be unable to get the information they need. By themselves, these points help explain the stunningly low take-up rates for many federal and state programs,[8] as well as the immense difficulty that people often have in obtaining permits or licenses of various sorts.[9] We should even see sludge as an obstacle to freedom, especially insofar as it reduces or impairs navigability.[10] If you cannot find your way through a fog, it makes sense to say that you are, to that extent, less free.

People are not, of course, perfectly rational. No reader of Shakespeare, Dickens, or Joyce, or observer of daily life, is unaware of this point. But decades of work on judgment and decision-making, coming from psychologists and behavioral economists, have specified how people depart from perfect rationality.[11] The relevant research has uncovered an assortment of biases to which most of us are subject. Those biases amplify the real-world effects of sludge. You might speculate that when the stakes are high—when real money is on the line—people won't be subject to behavioral biases. But that plausible speculation is wrong. Even when there are strong economic incentives, human beings do not behave as they should.[12]

For purposes of understanding the relationship between sludge and behavioral biases, a central point is that for many people, inertia is a powerful force.[13] We tend to keep doing what we are doing. In addition, people tend to procrastinate.[14] If they do not have to do something right now, they might plan to do it tomorrow, and when tomorrow comes, that will continue to be their plan. Even when people do have to do something right now, they might find a reason to delay. If people suffer from inertia and if they procrastinate, they might never do necessary paperwork. That is one reason that participation rates are typically much lower with opt-in designs than with opt-out designs.[15] When people are asked to opt into some program, the rate is often between 40 percent and 60 percent, even when it is an exceedingly beneficial program. Even a relatively modest amount of sludge can cut participation rates from 100 percent to under 50 percent.

The problem of inertia is compounded by *present bias*.[16] To many of us, the future seems like a foreign country—Laterland—and we are not sure that we will ever visit. It is tempting to put off administrative tasks until another day. That day may never come, even if the consequences of delay are quite serious.

Suppose in this light that under national regulations, individuals, small businesses, and start-ups must fill out certain forms in order to be eligible for important benefits or to avoid significant penalties. They might find the task daunting and not even try. Or they might sincerely intend to do what must be done, but if the task can be put off, or if it is burdensome or difficult, their behavior might not match their intentions. The actual costs might turn out to be very high; the perceived costs might be far higher. They might start and never finish. To get ahead of the story: it would make a lot sense for public officials to "scrub" existing paperwork burdens to make sure that they are not doing unintended or inadvertent harm. That is the idea of a Sludge Audit. The

2020 war on sludge, spurred by the coronavirus pandemic, is a case in point.

Scarcity and Sludge

There is a great deal of unlovely jargon within the executive branch of the US government. The product of an activity is called the *deliverable*. A task that follows a meeting is called a *do-out*. A request for action is described as the *ask*. If someone needs to continue a discussion with a colleague, she will promise to *circle back*. A person outside the government who will publicly approve of what the government is doing is called a *validator*. If a meeting with the president is canceled, it is *pulled down*. If a project must be abandoned or put on hold because of competing demands on people's time and attention, the problem is one of *bandwidth*. Of course, such terms can be found in many other places, including in businesses, but they are used with particular regularity in the White House itself.

Of the various unlovely terms, *bandwidth* is the most useful and the most interesting. The central idea is that public officials have the capacity to focus on, and to promote and implement, only a subset of the universe of good ideas. Bandwidth is limited partly for political reasons. In any particular period, members of Congress, executive branch officials, and the public itself may be unwilling to support more than a small set of proposals.

But much of the problem involves the limits of time and attention. A proposed reform might seem excellent, and it might even be able to attract considerable political support, but perhaps the minds of the people who might pursue it are occupied, and perhaps they do not have the time to learn about it and to explore its merits. Within government, some good ideas fail to go anywhere not because anyone opposes them, but because the system lacks the bandwidth to investigate them. As it turns out, the problem of sludge is a case in point.

Economists focus on the problem of scarcity—on how people allocate their resources (including both time and money) in the face of many competing demands. In an extraordinarily illuminating book, bearing directly on the effects of sludge, Sendhil Mullainathan and Eldar Shafir explore something quite different, which is the *feeling* of scarcity, and the psychological and behavioral consequences of that feeling.[17] The feeling of scarcity differs across various kinds of experiences. One can feel hungry, busy, lonely, or poor, and the consequences of those feelings are not the same. With respect to sludge, a central point is that in the face of cognitive scarcity, the navigation challenge is worse than daunting.

The feeling of scarcity puts people in a kind of cognitive tunnel, limiting what they are able to see. It depletes their self-control. It can make them more impulsive and sometimes a bit dumb. And by occupying the mind, scarcity can prevent people from attending to other matters, emphatically including sludge. If your mind is full, it will have a hard time handling new material. Social scientists have done many experiments involving *cognitive load*. In such experiments, they ask people to solve complex problems and then test whether the effort affects their behavior in other respects—for example, by leading them to choose chocolate cake over fruit. A standard finding is that their self-control is diminished; they are more likely to go for the cake. Scarcity works in the same way. It imposes a kind of "bandwidth tax" that impairs people's ability to perform well. Sludge imposes that kind of tax, and when people are already facing high taxes, they cannot easily handle more.

In an experiment that illuminates the adverse effects of sludge, Mullainathan and Shafir asked a group of people to imagine that their car needed to be fixed, that the repair would cost $300, and that they were making a choice between getting it fixed immediately or waiting (and hoping that the car might work for a while longer). Then the authors asked: How would you make this decision? Would it be an easy or hard decision to make? After receiving people's answers, the authors asked them a series of questions of the sort that appear on conventional intelligence tests. Well-off people and poor people did not show any difference in intelligence.

In a second version of the experiment, the authors posed exactly the same problem, but with a single difference: the cost of the repair was $3,000 rather than $300. Here is the remarkable finding: After encountering the second version of the problem, poor people did significantly worse than well-off people on the same intelligence test. What explains the difference? The answer is not more challenging arithmetic. When the authors posed nonfinancial problems, the use of small or large numbers produced no difference between poor people and rich people. Nor did the problem involve a lack of motivation. When the authors paid people for correct answers (and thus gave poor people an especially strong incentive to do well), the $3,000 version continued to create a large difference between poor people and well-off people on general intelligence questions.

For people without a lot of money, it is extremely challenging to try to figure out a way to come up with $3,000. To meet that challenge, they have to think extremely hard, which is depleting, and which makes it harder to do well on subsequent tasks. After people are depleted in that way, they do worse on intelligence tests. Mullainathan and Shafir replicated their general result with sugarcane farmers in India, finding that they do far worse on intelligence tests before a harvest, when they have little money and are preoccupied with how to make ends meet, than after a harvest, when cash is plentiful. Stunningly, the effect of plentiful cash was equivalent to a nine- to ten-point boost in IQ.

A depletion of bandwidth also reduces people's capacity for self-control. After being asked to try to remember eight-digit numbers, people are more likely to be rude in difficult social situations. The general lesson is that when people's attention is absorbed by other matters, they are more likely to yield to their impulses. With this lesson in mind, Mullainathan and Shafir insist that certain characteristics that we attribute to individual personality (lack of motivation, inability to focus) may actually be a problem of limited bandwidth. The problem is scarcity, not the person. Compare a computer that is working slowly because a lot of other programs are operating in the background. Nothing is wrong with the computer; you just need to turn off the other programs.

Scarcity tends to produce more of the same. For example, most of us are susceptible to the *planning fallacy*, which means that we are unrealistically optimistic about how long it will take to complete a project. By definition, busy people face a particular problem of cognitive scarcity, because they are attending to their current projects and so are more distracted. The underlying problem is that when people "tunnel," they focus on their immediate problem. When they are doing that, how likely is it that they will find their way through sludge?

To understand the point, it is useful to consider the words of the economist Esther Duflo, Nobel Prize winner and one of the world's leading experts on poverty:[18]

> We tend to be patronizing about the poor in a very specific sense, which is that we tend to think, "Why don't they take more responsibility for their lives?" And what we are forgetting is that the richer you are the less responsibility you need to take for your own life because everything is taken care [of] for you. And the poorer you are the more you have to be responsible for everything about your life. . . . Stop berating people

> for not being responsible and start to think of ways
> instead of providing the poor with the luxury that
> we all have, which is that a lot of decisions are taken
> for us. If we do nothing, we are on the right track. For
> most of the poor, if they do nothing, they are on the
> wrong track.

The problem of finding the right track is more serious for some people, and for some demographic groups, than it is for others. For those who are busy, sick, poor, disabled, taking care of small children, or elderly, cognitive scarcity is a special challenge. That conclusion clarifies the importance of focusing on the distributional effects of sludge—on whom sludge is most likely to hurt.[19]

For a glimpse of the distributional promise of sludge reduction, consider some research from the United Kingdom.[20] Starting in 2008, that nation adopted a policy of automatic enrollment in pension plans—one of the largest such reform efforts in the world. By making enrollment automatic, the new policy eliminated sludge. Before the reform, people with low levels of mental health were significantly less likely to participate in pension plans. The reform wiped out the disparity; it drove it down to zero. As the authors note, the finding is consistent with others, showing that automatic enrollment typically reduces the gaps in pension participation among low-income employees and also women.

The point is hardly limited to pension plans. The sludge-reduction effort during the coronavirus pandemic was motivated in part by a clear recognition of distributional issues. People without a lot of money, or struggling with illness or old age, were intended beneficiaries of many programs. If they had to run a gauntlet in order to get what they were entitled to, they might get it too late or not at all. The response was to cut sludge.

It is important to emphasize that as a practical matter, the victims of sludge are often the poorest among us. A central reason is that if you are poor, you have to focus on a wide range of immediately pressing problems.[21] If the government is asking poor people to navigate a complex system or to fill out a lot of forms, they might be especially likely to give up. But the problem is not limited to the poor. When programs are designed to benefit the elderly, sludge might be especially damaging—certainly if the population suffers from reduced cognitive capacity.

For different reasons, the problem of sex equality deserves particular attention.[22] Because women do a disproportionate amount of administrative work—running the household, arranging meals, taking care of children—a significant reduction in sludge could address a pervasive source of social inequality, with ramifying effects on other areas of life.

3
Sludge as Architecture

We have seen enough to know that seemingly small amounts of sludge can have large consequences—a clear demonstration of the effects of "choice architecture" in determining outcomes.[1] Choice architecture is the background against which decisions are made. Consider the layout of a grocery store (what's at eye level? what do you see when you enter?); the design of a website (what's in large font?); applications for permits and loans. Sludge is part of choice architecture. A store can impose some sludge before you buy cigarettes or e-cigarettes; perhaps you have to show identification and fill out some forms. A website can create some sludge to discourage you from selecting certain options. Applications can be so long and complicated that some people, or many people, will not bother.

Choice architecture can be pervaded by sludge or can be nearly free of it. Companies are well aware of that point. When they want you to choose an option, they make it really easy. They take away the sludge. With one click, you do what they want you to do. *Dark patterns* online—understood as manipulative practices designed to trick people into parting with their money—consist in large part of selective decreases and increases in sludge.

I have noted that in many domains, participation rates can be dramatically increased with a mere shift from requiring people to apply (opt in) to automatically enrolling them (opt out) and thus eliminating sludge. In an especially dramatic study, Professors Peter Bergman of Columbia University and Todd Rogers of Harvard University found that if parents are asked whether they want to sign up to receive text message alerts about the academic progress of their children, participation rates are tiny—around 1 percent.[2] If the sign-up process is simplified, participation rates increase significantly, to about 8 percent.[3] But if parents are automatically signed up, participation rates jump to 96 percent![4] An opt-out process is essentially an elimination of sludge, and with an opt-out approach, we can often achieve important social goals, whether we are interested in education, reduction of poverty, consumer protection, or climate change.

To be sure, most changes in choice architecture do not have effects of that magnitude.[5] If you switch from opt in to opt out, the standard increase in participation has been found to be around 26 percent. But that is a lot. More generally, simplification and sludge reduction do not merely reduce frustration; they change people's lives.

Successful Architecture

The right to vote may be the most fundamental of all, and it is often compromised by sludge. Here is a small example of how new or different architecture can help. The example has everything to do with overcoming the bandwidth problem.[6]

For millions of Americans, the steps needed to understand the process of where and how to become registered, and then following those steps, operate as serious barriers to voting. One result is that the nation ends up with stark demographic differences with respect to voter registration. In 2016, for example, a disproportionately large share of eligible Americans who were not registered were low-income citizens and people of color.[7]

Among eligible voters, 31 percent of African Americans, 43 percent of Hispanics, and just over 43 percent of low-income Americans were not registered to vote in the 2016 presidential election. When asked why they had not registered to vote, more than 60 percent of eligible voting-age adults responded that they had simply never been offered the chance to register.[8] And more than one-third of those not registered said that they intended to do so, but had not gotten around to it or found the process inconvenient.

Hospitals can play a role in closing this gap by offering citizens a chance to register to vote in a place where poor people, and people of color, disproportionately show up for care: the emergency room. In that way, hospitals can reduce sludge. Emergency rooms care for higher rates of low-income, minority, and uninsured Americans than the average population. In 2016, for example, the annual visit rate among the entire population was 45.8 ER visits per one hundred persons.[9] But when stratified among African American patients, the ER visit rate was much higher: eighty visits per one hundred persons. In addition, people without a college education and with lower incomes are especially reliant on the ER for nonemergency care.

While this illustrates a problem in our current medical system, it also introduces an opportunity to increase voter registration. Patients coming in for low-acuity complaints are more likely to wait while ER hospital staff care for other patients who have more urgent problems. The waits can be for four to six hours. If someone is having acute chest pain, obviously it is not the time to think about voter registration. But if people are asking for a strep test and would likely have to wait for several hours to be seen, that time could be leveraged. Why not ask patients if they want to use approximately ninety seconds of their waiting time to register to vote?

There is precedent for doing something like that. In 2008, the National Association of Community Health Centers ran a voter registration drive in health centers where patients received care. The result was that more than eighteen thousand low-income and middle-income citizens were added to the official rolls. Another program, conducted in 2012 at two Federally Qualified

Health Centers in the Bronx, New York, showed that a large number of voters could be registered easily without requiring significant physician effort, creating undue political influence, or compromising patient-doctor relationships.

Many unregistered voters are highly receptive to the prospect of being offered a chance to register, with one study finding an 89 percent agreement rate among those approached in a hospital waiting room and asked whether or not they would be open to registering to vote.[10] Hospitals have been initiating efforts to increase voter registration, such as MGH Votes, a campaign launched at Massachusetts General Hospital.[11] MGH also adopted a program called VotER,[12] which essentially eliminates sludge for voter registration, with a simple kiosk that allows registration in a very short time. That program has been duplicated in many other hospitals. Extending the VotER program to emergency rooms in general has extraordinary promise, and for one reason above all: it engages Americans who are not registered to vote by meeting them exactly where they are.

There are plenty of other ways to protect people's voting rights by reducing sludge. Voting by mail eliminates what some people consider to be the burdens of getting to the polls and standing in line. So long as the risk of fraud can be contained (and current evidence suggests that it can), voting by mail is an excellent way to cut sludge with respect to a right that is central to self-government.

Federal law requires states to send mail-in forms (return cards) before purging voters from electoral rolls on change-of-residence grounds (if a voter has not already confirmed a move).[13] That's good; it reduces the risk of unjustified purges. At the same time, each state is allowed to choose its own trigger for sending the return card. Some states use change-of-address information provided by the US Postal Service, but others use methods that can very foreseeably flag voters who have in fact not moved and thus remain eligible.[14] For example, a qualified voter can be struck for failing to mail the return card back and not voting for four years.[15] Voters—along with Congress and the Supreme Court—may be optimistic that they will do that, but their optimism is almost certainly misplaced.[16] Having to mail that card back is a form of sludge, and some people might forget to do so.

I will return to voting rights and sludge in chapter 4. The only point here is that the architecture for voting and voting registration can contain a lot of sludge or a little, and for the democratic process, the amount greatly matters.

Architecture and Architects

In many contexts, sludge is produced by architects who know exactly what they are doing. But in other contexts, sludge has a significant impact that architects do not foresee. Many of them are unrealistically optimistic

about the likelihood that people will overcome inertia. Even specialists are surprised at the extent to which
apparently promising strategies for defeating sludge turn
out to fail. For example, people might be reminded about
what they have to do, but they might ignore reminders.
In the private sector, sludge is used opportunistically by
clever marketers who seek to give consumers the impres-
sion that they will receive an excellent deal but who know
that people will not read the fine print or take advantage
of an available opportunity.[17]

In government, sludge might have a damaging effect
that public officials do not anticipate. In particular, officials might not understand the extent to which sludge
will adversely affect a population that they are seeking
to help. I can report, from personal experience (and as a
lawyer), that lawyers are often the problem here. They
impose sludge with the belief that it really is not much
of a problem. Surely people can fill out a four-page form?
Surely they can answer questions about their employment history and their places of residence over the past
fifteen years? Maybe so, but maybe not, and maybe it is
a lot harder than we lawyers think. Something similar
can be said of the private sector—which is a reason that
businesses, nonprofits, and educational institutions can
benefit from Sludge Audits.

But no one should doubt that sometimes public officials impose sludge on purpose. They know exactly what
they are doing. They are self-conscious choice architects,
fully cognizant of the impact of sludge. They might agree

to some costly program, designed to help poor people. But they might not love that program. They use sludge as a way of reducing costs or decreasing the real-world impact of the program. They are entirely aware that they are doing that. Sludge might be part of the price of a program designed to protect a vulnerable group that does not have a lot of political power. The program itself might seem exceedingly generous. But in the fine print, you can find the sludge.

In many cases, government officials are responding to political values and commitments, and they are not hiding anything. They impose sludge to reduce costs, to ensure that licensees are properly qualified, or to prevent benefits from going to people who do not really need or deserve them—points to which I will return.

In the private sector, similar things happen. Sludge might be a way of ensuring that people really qualify for something—say, a mortgage. Or it might be a self-serving effort to make relevant terms incomprehensible; if you have to wade through lengthy and complex materials, you might not understand key provisions.[18] In some of the worst cases, people are automatically subjected to certain terms or conditions, or to certain economic obligations, without consenting in any meaningful sense; sludge is the basic problem. There is a good argument in favor of a new right: *the right not to be manipulated.* Sludge can be the mechanism by which that right is violated. And when the public sector uses sludge to manipulate people, something has gone badly wrong.

I have referred to the idea of *dark patterns*, which have been defined as "user interface design choices that benefit an online service by coercing, steering, or deceiving users into making unintended and potentially harmful decisions."[19] Dark patterns come from both public and private institutions. The category goes well beyond sludge. Deception and steering need not involve sludge. People could, for example, be nudged into making harmful choices, as when a costly or harmful path or outcome is made especially easy (a kind of dark pattern). In such cases, sludge may not be involved. *Shrouded attributes*, such as add-on costs, might be self-consciously hidden from consumers, but it is fair to question whether they count as sludge.[20] Probably we should say that sludge is involved insofar as consumers have to do real work to learn about those attributes.

However we answer that question, a lot of dark patterns involve sludge, and they are very dark.

4
Sludge in Action

It would be valuable to catalog an assortment of programs that have been adversely affected, to varying degrees, by sludge. Ideally, such a catalog would be global rather than national. Focusing on the United States, I will offer a mere sketch here, limited to four areas: benefits programs, occupational licensing, student visas, and fundamental rights. Some of the discussion will borrow from a superb treatment by Professors Pamela Herd and Donald Moynihan, whose extraordinary book, *Administrative Burden*, offers a series of case studies of the effects of administrative burdens.[1] That treatment is relatively comprehensive, and because the situation is constantly shifting and varies from nation to nation, we need much more like it. My modest goal here is to illustrate the problem and to draw some broader lessons.

The central point is simple. In some contexts, sludge is a serious problem, but in others, the government has ensured that it is negligible. It would be valuable to offer a similar sketch for the private sector, showing (for example) that some businesses minimize sludge for customers and that others maximize it. Broadly speaking, that sketch would look a lot like this one.[2] For example, many companies make people spend a great deal of time and effort to cancel subscriptions. They hide relevant terms so that people have to wade through sludge to find them. They make certain terms essentially unintelligible to most consumers. For every use of sludge discussed here, there is a business analog. Sludge is often a form of manipulation; as we have seen, it is a component of dark patterns, especially online. But as in government, so too in the private sector: some of the harms of sludge are inadvertent, a result of paying too little attention to the problem.

Benefit Programs

Social Security

With respect to sludge, a model program is Social Security, which is simple and in many ways automatic—something close to a sludge-free zone. As Herd and Moynihan put it, "the biggest bookkeeping organization in the world banished burdens."[3] The US government takes care of a lot of what might have been turned into sludge, and it generally requires citizens to do very little. One reason is that the Social Security Administration (SSA) tracks peoples' earnings and determines eligibility and benefit levels automatically. If you are eligible, you can enroll online or go to one of the nation's 1,200 field offices.[4] After you do that, you are likely to receive direct deposits into your bank account within a month.[5] In fact, Social Security can be seen as a kind of model. Dealing with an older population, it puts few demands on recipients. It operates a bit like modern departments of motor vehicles, which automatically renew drivers' licenses after a few clicks and send them in the mail. For many retirees, the money comes with hardly any friction.

As a matter of history, there is a large irony here. In the 1930s, the supposed administrative challenge was taken as a serious objection to the very idea of Social Security.[6] But the federal government succeeded in meeting that challenge. It did so in part through the creation and use of Social Security numbers, which make it much simpler to track people's earnings over their entire working lives.[7] The SSA has worked hard and mostly successfully to make things easy for beneficiaries, replacing lost Social Security cards, taking applications, updating records, and ensuring the accuracy of payments.[8] For beneficiaries, the program is generally working. The poverty rate among older adults is now just 9 percent; if Social Security were not included in their income, it would be 40 percent.[9] Almost one-third of beneficiaries rely on the program for at least 90 percent of their income.[10]

Other programs also show high take-up rates, in large part because of low levels of sludge. A prime example is Medicare Part A, for which individuals are automatically enrolled upon application for Social Security retirement or disability benefits.[11] Data from the early 2000s, on which the US Department of Health and Human

Services relied for an Issue Brief in 2012, indicates that Medicare Part A features a 99 percent take-up rate.[12] (Note here the spectacular results of automatic enrollment.) Medicare Parts B and D are not too far behind, at 96 and 93 percent, respectively.[13]

Earned Income Tax Credit

The level of sludge is also relatively low for the Earned Income Tax Credit (EITC), a wage subsidy for low-income workers.[14] Most programs designed to benefit poor people have dispiriting take-up rates of between 30 and 60 percent; for the EITC, the rate is about 80 percent.[15] That is excellent news, for the EITC ranks among the most effective of US antipoverty programs. Because it makes work more remunerative, it significantly increases labor force participation.[16] The EITC also makes a major dent in the national poverty rate and helps children in particular, with beneficial effects on their health, their cognitive abilities, and their long-term educational prospects.[17]

For the EITC, the relatively high take-up rate is a product of relatively low levels of sludge. The paperwork requirements are modest; a standard tax return is all that is necessary. The Internal Revenue Service (IRS) sends simple, clear reminders to people who appear to be eligible, and the reminders significantly increase participation rates.[18] In that way, it helps to overcome the problem of cognitive scarcity. The IRS also runs voluntary programs that provide free tax help. Because participation involves little in the way of frustration or stigma, the psychological costs are low.

To be sure, the EITC is not as simple or automatic as Social Security, and sludge reduction thus remains a high priority. If 20 percent of eligible people are not receiving a potentially life-changing benefit, there is a serious problem. The IRS almost certainly knows enough to enroll people automatically and send a refund to eligible taxpayers, and that is probably what it should be doing.[19] Nonetheless, the administrative burdens for recipients are much lower than they might be.

It is reasonable to ask: Why? In the context of Social Security, national politicians had strong incentives to reduce sludge, and a lot of older people depend on the money, which means that there is a politically powerful group in favor of sludge reduction. For the EITC, the secret of relative success is an unlikely coalition between business interests and those seeking to help the working poor.[20] Business interests much like the EITC because it creates an incentive for low-wage work. Those who care about the working poor like the EITC because it makes the working poor less poor. The two interests have been able to work together—not to make the program as generous as it might be, but at least to reduce sludge.

Supplemental Nutrition Assistance Program

Unfortunately, many benefits programs impose more daunting burdens. The Supplemental Nutrition Assistance

Program (SNAP), formerly known as the Food Stamps Program (FSP), provides nutritional in-kind benefits for low-income families.[21] It is the largest nutritional program in the United States, serving more than thirty-five million people per month and providing average monthly benefits of roughly $130 per person.[22] SNAP has been shown to improve food security and improve the well-being of children in participating families.[23] To be eligible, applicants must have a gross monthly household income within 130 percent of the national poverty line and also a net monthly household income (after deductions of, for example, housing and childcare) within 100 percent of the national poverty line. In addition, household assets must be below a certain threshold.[24]

In comparison with other social assistance programs, SNAP has a relatively high participation rate.[25] The USDA estimated the SNAP annual monthly participation rate as 85 percent in 2016.[26] Even so, a significant percentage of the eligible population does not receive SNAP benefits. One reason is sludge.[27]

Significant levels of sludge can be found in both the application and the recertification processes. The USDA has concluded that different levels of sludge were a large contributor to differences in participation rates across states.[28] One study found that the average SNAP application took more than five hours to complete. It included two trips to the local office and out-of-pocket application costs that averaged about $10.31. A survey found that most application forms were more than ten pages long and included warnings of high fines and jail time if people made erroneous statements on their form.[29] Application forms may include obscure questions, asking applicants whether they own a prepaid burial plot (twenty-nine states), whether they sell blood (two states), or whether they have any bingo winnings (one state)—and affirmative answers require documentation.[30]

The good news is that forty-seven states have adopted online applications, and many have switched to allowing phone interviews. At the same time, applicant responses have been mixed.[31] On the government side, decision processes can be slow, thus delaying or preventing the receipt of needed benefits. A study finds that people who experience monthly food shortfalls due to seasonal unemployment often do not receive their benefits within the thirty-day mandated application decision window—and by the time a decision is reached, they no longer require the benefits.[32]

All this should be sufficient to show that for many people, the application itself can be challenging to complete.[33] Recertification also imposes sludge on applicants. To remain in the program, recipients must prove eligibility in specified time intervals that vary by state. Frequently, they lose program benefits and must reapply, creating significant costs for both administrators and recipients.[34] In California's SNAP program (CalFresh), recipients must complete an interview by the end of the calendar month in which their recertification period ends; if they fail to do so, they lose their benefits.[35]

Interviews are randomly assigned across the month, which means that some participants have up to four weeks to complete postinterview requirements, while others have only a few days.[36]

An important study found that the timing of the assigned interview had a significant impact on recertification success, with each day later in the month producing a 0.33 percent increase in recertification failure as opposed to the previous day.[37] Especially important was the opportunity to reschedule missed appointments; that opportunity was of course significantly reduced if recipients were assigned an interview at the end of the month. While many of the recipients who initially fail are eventually recertified, some are not and permanently leave the program.

The increased sludge introduced by recertification processes often screens out the neediest households and decreases targeting efficiency.[38] In response, some states have tried to make recertification procedures easier. But their effort has been complicated by state-level administrative processes that can penalize states for issuing benefits to people who are not eligible. Those processes have led states to adopt stricter standards and procedures for both recertification and application.[39]

Temporary Assistance for Needy Families

Temporary Assistance for Needy Families (TANF) is a block grant, which in 1996 replaced Aid to Families with Dependent Children (AFDC) as the main federally funded cash assistance program for poor families with children.[40] TANF's estimated participation rate has dropped every year since it was enacted, from a high of 69 percent of eligible households in 1996 to just 25 percent in 2016.[41] In 2018, TANF reached merely twenty-two of every one hundred families with children living in poverty nationwide.[42] Sixteen states had a TANF-to-poverty ratio of less than ten in 2018, meaning that for every one hundred families living in poverty, ten or fewer receive TANF cash assistance. Most of those states are situated in the South and Southeast. In comparison, California had a ratio of sixty-eight.[43] One result of these differences is a severe disparate impact on African American children, who disproportionally live in states with low TANF-to-poverty ratios.[44]

Sludge is a significant source of the problem. The application process for TANF can take a great deal of work. That process often involves lengthy application forms, in-person visits to distance offices, and a copious amount of supporting documentation.[45] In addition, TANF includes "work first" policies in many states, which require applicants to attend orientation sessions or at least to conduct a job search in advance of the eligibility determination.[46] New York City has had an especially complex application process; at one early stage, it included two eligibility interviews in different locations, a home visit by an agency staff member, a mandatory workforce orientation, and daily job search classes for thirty days.[47] Such requirements primarily keep two groups from participating: (1) people who would receive relatively few benefits and do not think the procedure is worth it and (2) people who face such serious social disadvantages that the requirements place an insuperable burden on them.[48]

As with SNAP, many states now allow online applications.[49] Unfortunately, many basic online application tools are still missing. For example, most states do not allow applicants to update information after the application is submitted or permit applicants to check their application status online.[50] Another form of sludge, particularly relevant for TANF in light of its work requirement rules, consists of limited business hours at welfare centers, which impose additional barriers on people who are working.

TANF eligibility rules are often complex, and they differ significantly from state to state. For these reasons, a lack of awareness of eligibility can be a major hurdle to participation.[51] Even if people know that they might be eligible, they might not know how to apply for benefits or might misunderstand key program rules.[52] Finding out about the rules and application procedures imposes learning costs, with disproportionate adverse effects on identifiable groups.[53] There is also evidence that many TANF recipients show present bias and therefore do not take account of sanctions based on cash-assistance time limits until it is too late.[54] A noteworthy aspect of TANF participation is the relatively low participation of eligible Hispanic parents.[55] The low participation rate might be a product of fears about the legal consequences of need-ing assistance; it might be related to misunderstandings about program eligibility for legal immigrants.[56]

The Affordable Care Act

For the Affordable Care Act (ACA),[57] sludge has been a major problem, and the human consequences have been severe. A primary goal of the ACA is to give people access to low-cost health insurance and, in the process, to ensure that people who have preexisting conditions or expensive health problems cannot be denied insur-ance. If the ACA operates as it was intended, it should make a massive dent in the size of the uninsured population. And by doing that, it should significantly improve health outcomes, reducing both morbidity and mortality.

In many ways, the ACA has indeed operated as it was intended. From the beginning, however, the federal sys-tem has created large-scale challenges, in part because of the volume of sludge. Sharply opposed to the very idea of Obamacare, twenty-seven states simply refused to adopt exchanges, which were supposed to provide people with a simple, relatively sludge-free way to buy health insurance.[58] As a result of that refusal, citizens in those states have not had exchanges at all. They have had to apply through federal exchanges, and that is usually more cumbersome. To summarize a long story: Successful applicants initially receive a notice from the federal government that they are eligible for the state

Medicaid program. The federal government then transfers the file to the state. After that, the state determines
eligibility.[59] This process can take months, and it has left
millions of people in limbo.

In the first years of the ACA, the Obama administration worked hard to reduce administrative burdens and
to eliminate sludge. It publicized the program in an effort
to increase the likelihood that people would know what
was available, and it also took aggressive steps to simplify
the enrollment process. From the standpoint of the law's
proponents, not nearly enough was done, but they saw
it as a start. By contrast, the subsequent administration,
unenthusiastic about the law as a matter of policy, took
steps in the opposite direction. For example, it reduced
funding for publicity. It shortened the sign-up period.[60]
It took a variety of other steps to decrease simplicity and
to ramp up the sludge.

In the program's initial years, participants in the ACA
who enrolled through federal exchanges were automatically re-enrolled in their plan if they did not notify relevant officials of eligibility changes or initiate action to
select a new plan. In February 2020, the Trump administration released a proposed rule that would end automatic re-enrollment for enrollees whose premiums were
fully paid by a tax credit and instead require those individuals to reselect their health insurance each year.[61]
The Center on Budget and Policy Priorities has urged that
this sludge-producing change would disproportionately
hurt low-income enrollees.[62]

When HealthCare.gov was initially launched in October 2013, it encountered an assortment of problems, creating a national controversy. In short, the site did not work. Public officials immediately made substantial improvements, eliminating the main problems, cutting sludge, and greatly easing navigation. The ACA itself created Navigator programs that provide outreach, education, and in-person assistance to people attempting to obtain access to the site. Such in-person services give people a helpful tutor for navigating the sludge. In a sense, they are sludge-busters. They also provide more personalized advice than the website or hotlines might be able to provide. For example, a Navigator can help people to determine whether a family member temporarily sleeping on their couch qualifies as a tax dependent.[63]

The 2013 budget for the Navigator programs was $100 million, but the Trump administration reduced that number to just $10 million in 2017.[64] It is difficult to know the precise effects of the cuts, but with greatly reduced funding, outreach and educational activities have had to be scaled back. At the same time, in-person assistance has been reduced. A likely result is that fewer people were able to sign up for coverage.[65]

During the Obama administration, the federal government itself did a great deal to publicize the availability of health insurance. Among other things, it directly reached out to people via email, encouraging them to sign up or re-enroll. During the Trump administration, these activities were much reduced. In November 2017, for example, the relevant department sent emails with sign-up options only to people with current healthcare plans. It declined to email others listed in the government's database of some twenty million people who had coverage at some point or who had explored HealthCare.gov.[66] The result was to leave many people unaware of their options or reliant on their own research (or the reduced number of public ACA advertisements). Here, then, is a situation in which information costs amount to a form of sludge.

The ACA offered states a financial incentive to expand Medicaid eligibility, and thirty-seven states accepted.[67] All states permit people to qualify for Medicaid based on a set of factors, including income, household size, disability, and family status. The expansion permits people in relevant states to qualify on the basis of income alone.[68] In an effort to limit the reach of the program, the Trump administration urged states to adopt work requirements for Medicaid beneficiaries, who have to submit additional paperwork to demonstrate that they are employed or in school.[69]

Meeting these work requirements has proved to be particularly challenging for some Medicaid beneficiaries. Nationwide, nearly 80 percent of potentially eligible beneficiaries live with a worker, despite not working themselves. In Arkansas, the first state to impose a work requirement,[70] more than three-quarters of enrollees subject to the new work requirement had no access to a vehicle, no internet access, less than a high school education, a serious health limitation, or a household member with a serious health limitation.[71] Despite these barriers, many in fact had jobs, but simply did not meet the hours requirement in order to qualify for Medicaid.[72]

The real sludge came when those who actually met the requirement struggled to report it through their state's online system. First, many in Arkansas's program lacked a personal computer at home, so they had to borrow friends' computers or obtain access to the online portal through a public library.[73] Second, sludge-filled websites made it difficult to obtain access to Medicaid reporting accounts and understand what to report. One participant reported, "I had to use a friend's computer and they had to help me . . . they are pretty smart and it took us over 10 and a half hours just to set [my account] up in the first place."[74]

Medicare

Medicare is a nearly universal program aimed at older people.[75] As noted, those who are eligible for Social Security are usually eligible for Medicare too, which means that in terms of enrollment, things are pretty simple. Nonetheless, Medicare has a great deal of sludge, which comes from the highly complex process faced by Medicare enrollees when choosing among services. What is the right supplemental insurance plan? What is the right prescription drug plan? Is a Medicare Advantage Plan a good idea? These are difficult questions, and older adults often suffer from cognitive decline.[76] Herd and Moynihan quote a Medicare beneficiary who notes, "That's what gets me, they wait until we retire to make it complicated."[77]

A great deal of behavioral evidence finds that Medicare beneficiaries are making poor choices and losing money in the process.[78] For that reason, there is a good argument that the government should simplify the process with the use of online tools, telephone assistance (with shorter waiting times), and customized recommendations.[79] It would be easy to imagine a nearly sludge-free process for people who prefer automaticity, accompanied by a more complex and informationally demanding process available to people who would like to make their own choices.

Occupational Licensing

To begin work, many people are required to obtain licenses. It seems reasonable to say that people cannot be architects, teachers, or nurses unless they receive some kind of certification. But what do they have to do, exactly? Across different professions and regions, the burdens of occupational licensing greatly vary. But in many cases, they are far too high. The sludge is overwhelming. It has serious adverse effects on people's lives. A whole book could (and should) be written on this topic. I touch on a few highlights here.

On average, occupational licenses in the United States require 248 hours of coursework.[80] They also require people to have some sort of experience before they can begin to work. A survey of licensure requirements, measuring burdens for 102 lower-income occupations, found that, on average, licensing laws require nearly a year of education and experience.[81]

Some occupations have unusually onerous requirements, and some of the comparisons seem anomalous. Becoming an interior designer takes an average of 2,190 days, which is higher than the number required to be a public school preschool teacher (2,050 days).[82] Other professions with onerous requirements include carpenter/cabinet maker contractor (licensed in thirty states with an average of 368 days); shampooer (thirty-seven states; 248 days); and tree trimmer (seven states; 574 days).[83]

Some states also require a great deal of paperwork. For cosmetology alone, the South Dakota Cosmetology Commission's website lists sixteen different forms, though some of them pertain only to specific requests and accommodations.[84]

The problem of long processing times for occupational licenses frequently arises in the context of interstate labor migration, when workers moving from one state to another state try to obtain a credential in their new home state to continue working in thier profession. This problem affects military spouses in particular, who often need to move around the country. In 2018, the US Department of Homeland Security and the US Department of Defense compiled a table of processing times for occupational licenses in various professions when cross-ing state lines.[85] The processing time is often a matter of months, and in some states it can be close to a year.

Student Visas

Many students want to study in the United States, and when they succeed, the benefits are substantial—not only for them, but for the United States itself. Any particular estimate of those benefits will be based on contestable assumptions, but according to one study, international students contributed over $41 billion to the US economy during the 2018–2019 academic year and supported almost 460,000 jobs.[86] Competition for the global international student population can be intense, and many countries have worked hard to increase their appeal as study destinations. China (9 percent of total international students in 2019), Canada (8 percent), and Australia (5 percent) all have significantly grown their market share, while the United States dropped from 28 percent of global international students in 2001 to 21 percent as of 2019.[87]

Let's bracket large-scale policies, produced, for exam-ple, by the COVID-19 pandemic and by the policies of the Trump administration, which has not been enthusi-astic about international students. Why did that num-ber decline over a relatively long period? One study finds that the sludge-filled visa application process is a principal contributor.[88] In a 2015 poll of prospective international students, the United States was ranked the very worst on visa procedures, with over 50 percent of respondents agreeing that it had "difficult or complex visa procedures."[89]

To understand the problem, it is useful to identify the three primary visa classes through which foreign students may legally study in the United States: (1) the F visa, (2) the M visa, and (3) the J visa. The F and the M visa programs are managed by the Student and Exchange Visitor Program (SEVP), which is part of the Department of Homeland Security (DHS), while the J visa program is managed by the Department of State (DOS).[90]

Of these, the most important is the F visa class, intended for "nonimmigrants whose primary purpose is to complete an academic course of study at an SEVP-certified school or program." In terms of sheer numbers, it is the most popular by far, with almost 390,000 new visas issued in 2019[91] and more than 1.55 million students with active status in 2018 (in combination with M visa students). The M-1 visa is similar to the F-1, with one key difference: the M-1 applies to students enrolled in a vocational course of study, rather than an academic course of study. Only 9,227 M-1 visas were issued in 2019, and 291 visas were issued for the student's dependents under the M-2 classification.[92] The J-1 visa includes people who are participating in an exchange visitor program meant to promote cultural exchange. While this category includes many students and scholars, it is a broader visa class, which also covers, for example, au pairs, interns, and government visitors. Including the J-2 (for dependents of J-1 visa holders), there were just over 390,000 J visas issued in 2019.[93]

The main source of sludge in the application process is the complexity and sheer number of forms and administrative burdens. For example, a normal F-1 visa application process involves at least the following steps:[94]

1. The prospective student must provide the university with a "source of support" form, demonstrating that she has sufficient funds to support her studies (this may include additional sheets for dependents). Information must be confirmed through official letters from multiple sources, such as banks and sponsors, and any currency amounts must be shown in US dollars. This process can take a lot of time, especially if the student is required to compile information from a variety of sources.

2. Upon receipt of the information, the relevant university must prepare the I-20 form and send it to the international student. This process can take two to three weeks.

3. After the student receives the I-20, she must pay the SEVIS fee of $350 to register in the visa online registration system and fill out form I-901 (blissfully, a short, single-page form). Most students can do this electronically—with the exception of those born in certain African countries, who must pay the fee and

send the form per money order to the United States. The fee is not refundable, even if the visa is later denied.[95]

4. After the student has received the SEVIS fee payment receipt, she must fill in the actual visa application form (called form DS-160) online. The DS-160 is a lengthy and detailed form, which takes around ninety minutes to complete, as estimated by the US Department of State.[96] For many students, that estimate might be optimistic. The form requires, for example, flight details of the student's previous five visits to the United States (regardless of how long ago in the past), employment information, past visa information, family information (such as the occupation and education of parents), and other biographical data, including information about the student's social media accounts. Users have reported frequent issues with website time-outs, causing them to lose information already typed in and requiring multiple restarts.

    Students must also pay a nonrefundable application fee of $160 (a different fee from the previously mentioned SEVIS fee).[97] Payment of this fee is sometimes not possible through a credit card online, and methods vary widely across countries (in Singapore, for example, payments are made through the local post office).[98]

    Many international students find it challenging to comply with the specifications of the DS-160 photo.

Because the requirements are quite detailed and extensive, and also differ from normal passport pictures, applicants may be required to visit an embassy-recommended professional studio to take the picture, which costs additional time and money.[99]

5. Once a student has submitted a DS-160, she may then schedule an interview at a US embassy or consulate. That may take up to several weeks. Visiting times at the US embassy vary widely and can take from a few hours to almost an entire day (the embassy in London, for example, estimates an average of two to three hours of waiting time).[100] The visit itself will also involve a security screening and the taking of the student's fingerprints prior to the interview.[101] Visitors are not allowed to carry their cell phones or other electronic devices.[102] The interview itself usually takes only a few minutes and often focuses on the students' ability to finance their stay in the United States and their commitment to return after their studies to their home country.

After the completion of the interview, the applicant is usually informed immediately about whether the visa has been granted or denied.[103] Once the visa has been denied, there is no recourse, unless new information is presented and the procedure is restarted. It is possible, however, that the responsible officer will determine that the application warrants "further administrative processing," which usually occurs when the applicant appears in certain databases (e.g., prior visa overstays, security risks). This may require the student to submit additional information and can extend the visa processing time significantly. In 2019, the allowed time for administrative processing was extended from 60 days to 180 days.[104]

In sum: The normal application process involves at least four different forms, two separate payments totaling $510 (with different payment rules and restrictions), and at least one visit to a US embassy, which is typically located only in large urban centers. The entire process takes at least one to two months under normal conditions. There is also a significant chance that a visa will be rejected. In 2019, for example, more than 25 percent of F-1 visa applications were rejected.[105]

This summary of the sludge encountered by international students in the United States is not exhaustive. Nor is it meant to suggest that the relevant burdens should be reduced by 75 percent, or 50 percent, or 25 percent, or even 10 percent. Most of them serve legitimate purposes; some of them are undoubtedly designed to discourage people from trying. But the question remains: How many of them could survive some kind of cost-benefit test?

Constitutional Rights

We have seen that sludge raises serious free speech issues. It can also endanger religious liberty, protection of private property, and rights in the criminal justice system.

I focus on two issues here because of their contemporary relevance and complexity: abortion and voting. One reason for their complexity is that with respect to those issues, reasonable people can take different views about sludge. This is true in the context of abortion because of moral disagreement. In the context of voting rights, there remain unsettled questions about how much sludge is necessary to ensure against voter fraud.

Abortion

Under current law, states are allowed to regulate the abortion right so long as their regulations do not impose an "undue burden."[106] Because that standard has a degree of vagueness, it can be taken to invite states to take steps to discourage abortion by imposing sludge. They have enthusiastically taken up the invitation.[107] For example, states have required pregnant women to engage in mandatory counseling, which includes descriptions not only of the procedure but also of fetal pain. They have required women to take and see an ultrasound, to make multiple visits to clinics, and to undergo significant waiting periods.[108] Some states impose a waiting period of seventy-two hours after a woman has seen her doctor. Some states require women to hear a mandatory "script," designed to discourage abortion.[109] These requirements impose evident costs in terms of time, necessary learning, and feelings of stigma and perhaps humiliation.

Imposition of sludge is now a preferred method for discouraging exercise of the abortion right. As noted, whether that is a good or bad thing depends on one's moral commitments. We might be dealing with reasonable, deliberation-promoting nudging in a domain in which the stakes are incalculably large; we might be dealing with excessive sludge in a domain in which the fundamental rights of women are at risk. But there is no question that sludge is being imposed.

To capture the qualitatively diverse costs, Herd and Moynihan offer an extensive quotation from a thirty-five-year-old woman, describing her experience of navigating administrative burdens in Wisconsin. Here is an excerpt:

> I am shaken. I am embarrassed. I am tired of waiting. I am now called into a room. I can bring Hubby this time. We are told to watch a video, again required by state law. The video talks about adoption, foster parenthood, the dangers of abortion, my rights. It drags on. I feel like a small child. Husband looks concerned and helpless. I sign a form indicating my understanding of the information presented on the video. We wait. A nurse finally comes back in. Time to go back to the waiting room. We'll call you in a short while.[110]

The sludge has had an impact. According to one study, sludge increases the cost of abortion by 19 percent and decreases the number of abortions by between 13 and 15 percent.[111] One consequence appears to be an increase in the incidence of self-administered abortions.[112] But for defenders of sludge in this context, there is a counterpoint. Consider the words of a woman who received an ultrasound as a donation from the Knights of Columbus, a Catholic fraternal service order:

> The only way I can describe it is that it changed me in the blink of an eye . . . The moment I saw my child on the big screen in front of me, I knew I was going to be a mom. It did not matter what I had thought before—all that mattered was loving my child and caring about her safety. I saw her little feet and little arms. I heard her heartbeat as I watched her in front of me. I still have the pictures of the ultrasound that were given to me that day—the day that changed my life forever.[113]

Voting

The Fifteenth Amendment to the US Constitution, forbidding denial of the vote "on account of race, color, or previous condition of servitude," was ratified in 1870, but sludge has long been used to disenfranchise African Americans. For decades, literacy tests were a favorite instrument; they were eventually forbidden by the Voting Rights Act of 1965. In recent years, sludge has often been reduced, in the sense that voting is often more convenient and registration is generally easier.[114] But sludge continues to exist, and in some states it is mounting. It is plainly being used as a political weapon, most prominently by Republican leaders seeking to impose sludge so as to increase their electoral prospects.[115]

Removing people from the rolls obviously creates sludge, because it forces people to take steps to reregister. At least one state permits people to be removed from the rolls for something as simple as not voting in the previous election. In 2017, Georgia's year-end total of voters purged from the rolls reached 660,000[116]—over 6 percent of Georgia's population (not considering the smaller number eligible to vote). Many states routinely "clean up" voter rolls to ensure that people who may have become ineligible to vote (e.g., by moving, by receiving a disenfranchising criminal conviction, or by death) are not permitted to remain on the rolls. That is perfectly legitimate, of course, but it may well result in numerous mistakes, which means that voters will have to face sludge. People may show up to vote only to be turned away or forced to file a provisional ballot.

According to a report from the Brennan Center, voter roll purges increased 33 percent nationwide from 2008 to 2018.[117] Some states are purging people who have not voted for a specified number of years or responded to a notice, thus requiring them to register again.[118] The New York City Board of Elections purged two hundred thousand voters in 2014 and 2015 for failing to update their forms, failing to vote since 2008, or moving (according to the National Change of Address database).[119] City officials notified voters of their removal but gave voters only fourteen days to respond before being automatically removed.[120]

Some states require state-issued photo identification.[121] That form of sludge might not seem particularly onerous, but according to some estimates, about 11 percent of Americans do not have a state-issued photo identification (including about 25 percent of African Americans).[122] Many college students may be effectively disenfranchised by voter ID laws. In North Carolina, student IDs, even from state institutions, were excluded from the list of acceptable ID forms until a court struck down the relevant law and new legislation was passed.[123]

Some states have also increased residency requirements and required proof of citizenship.[124] With respect to the right to vote, administrative burdens of multiple kinds are working to disenfranchise African Americans, the elderly, and people of low income.[125] Some of the most insidious forms of sludge involve dramatically reduced polling places and exceedingly long lines, sometimes requiring people to wait for up to seven hours before registering their vote. In some places, that burden is intentional. It is an effort to prevent particular people from voting.

How shall we put it? That is a disgrace. Many reforms could help. We have seen that automatic registration is an excellent idea. Voting by mail is another—especially, but not only, during or after a pandemic. A paid day off on election day is yet another.[126] Voting should be sludge-free.

5
Reasons for Sludge

Notwithstanding what I have said thus far, sludge often serves important goals. Sometimes it is indispensable. It saves money and even lives. It combats some of the worst human impulses, including recklessness, cruelty, selfishness, and greed. We can readily imagine six possible justifications for sludge:

1. Ensuring eligibility and program integrity
2. Counteracting self-control problems
3. Protecting privacy
4. Protecting security
5. Targeting benefits to those who most need or deserve them
6. Collecting important or even essential data

Each of these deserves extended discussion. None is going to get what it deserves. I will touch only on the essentials. As we will see, a great deal of sludge turns out to be justified, which means that the discussion in this chapter will provide a necessary sense of balance. In deciding whether to eliminate sludge, we need to know what sludge, exactly, we are talking about. Even so, the general point remains: there is far too much sludge out there.

Eligibility and Program Integrity

When public officials impose sludge, it is often because of a desire to ensure that programs work in the way that the law requires. One reason involves eligibility restrictions. Sludge can ensure that those restrictions are respected. People should not receive Medicare, Medicaid, the EITC, or Social Security unless they are entitled to the relevant benefits, and sludge is often a way of collecting necessary information. Even in the context of voting rights, burdens of various sorts can be and often are justified as a means of ensuring that would-be voters meet existing legal requirements. For spending programs, a usual justification for sludge points to "fraud, waste, and abuse";[1] sludge can be an effort to reduce all three.

Sludge is often imposed to obtain information about people's backgrounds—their employment history, their income, their criminal history (if any), their credit rating, their family history, their travel history, their places of residence. Those who seek to work in government, certainly at levels that involve national security, are required to provide a great deal of information of that sort.[2] (It takes endless hours, and some people do not provide all of the required information.) Would-be employees do not enjoy all the sludge. Nonetheless, it might well be justified. When students and others face administrative burdens to get visas, or to otherwise visit the United States, it may be to ensure compliance with legal requirements and to protect national security.

What is true for the public sector is true for the private sector as well. Banks and other institutions generate a lot of sludge. Those who seek a loan face sludge. A central reason is to ensure that they actually qualify. If you want to get a mortgage, you might find the process time-consuming, annoying, endless, and a bit humiliating. But banks do not want to give a lot of money to people who cannot pay it back. It is true that many companies try to obtain customers by keeping sludge to a minimum. But firms depends on sludge to make sure that they are enrolling or helping the right people. When patients encounter sludge at hospitals, it might be for good reasons.

It is true that with the increasing availability of information and with machine learning, private and public institutions might be able to find the relevant information on their own. In the private sector, some companies use the idea of *prequalification*, which means that they have enough information to know, in advance, that some people are already qualified for goods or services.[3] Sometimes forms can be prepopulated; as a result, forms might not be necessary.[4] That is a blessing, and the government should take far more advantage of it. In the domain of taxation, a dramatic example is the idea of *return-free filing*, which eliminates the need for taxpayers to fill out forms at all.[5] Some nations, such as Denmark, do that already. In the United States, reliance on return-free filing could save billions of hours in annual paperwork burdens. In the fullness of time, we should see significant movements in this direction.[6]

But those movements remain incipient. For the present and the near future, the most obvious justifications for sludge go by the name of *program integrity*.[7] Suppose that the IRS decided to send the EITC to apparently eligible taxpayers. If it could do so at low cost, and if the apparently eligible taxpayers are in fact eligible, there would be little ground for objection. The problem, of course, is the word *apparently*. It is possible that some of the recipients will not in fact be eligible. Whenever people are automatically enrolled in a program, some of them may not meet the legal criteria.

When this is so, public officials must choose between (1) a design ensuring that some eligible people will not receive a benefit and (2) a design ensuring that some ineligible people will receive a benefit. That may not be an easy choice, and it may not even be easy to decide on the criteria that we should use to make it. If the idea of program integrity is meant to refer to the number of errors, the choice between (1) and (2) might turn purely on arithmetic: Which group is larger? If automatic enrollment, removing the sludge, means that 500,000 eligible people will receive the benefit who otherwise would not, and if a degree of sludge means that 499,999 ineligible people will receive the benefit who otherwise would not, automatic enrollment might seem justified.

But it would be possible to see things differently. Suppose that automatic enrollment gives benefits to 200,000 eligible people but also to 200,100 ineligible people. Some people might think that if the 200,100 people are *nearly* eligible—if they are relatively poor—it is not so terrible if they receive some economic help. But other people might insist that taxpayer money is accompanied by clear restrictions and argue that if it is given out in violation of those restrictions, a grievous wrong has been committed. On this view, even a modest breach of program integrity, to the advantage of those who are not eligible, is unacceptable.

The most extreme version of this view would be that a grant of benefits to a very large number of eligibles would not outweigh the grant of benefits to a very small number of ineligibles. In my view, the most extreme version is hard to defend, unless the law requires it: a grant of benefits to a hundred people who are almost (but not quite) eligible is a price worth paying in exchange for a grant of benefits to a million people who are in fact eligible. But the correct trade-off is not self-evident, and reasonable people might differ.

The example might seem a bit tedious, but public officials encounter the problem all the time, and so do companies, universities, nonprofits, homeless shelters, hospitals, and others. As sludge increases, the class of people who receive a benefit may well include fewer who are not entitled to it. That's good. As sludge is reduced, there is an ever-growing risk that a benefit will go to people who should not be getting it. That's bad.

In some cases, of course, there is no need for sludge. We can obtain program integrity without it. In the direct certification program for school lunches, the level of accuracy appears to be very high; few ineligible children are allowed to qualify. It is increasingly possible to make things automatic, and so to eliminate sludge, without conferring benefits on the ineligible. The only point is that in many cases, trade-offs are inevitable, and different people can make different judgments.

Consider the question of voter registration. It would be great if we could eliminate sludge and make every eligible person a potential voter. Perhaps we can do that; as we have seen, the (excellent) idea of automatic voter registration is getting increasing support. Nonetheless, sludge has been defended as a way of combating the risk of fraud and thus ensuring the integrity of the voting process.[8] On imaginable assumptions, sludge reduction could have the benefit of ensuring that eligible people are allowed to vote while also having the cost of ensuring that the same is true of (some) ineligible voters. The size of the two categories surely matters.

Self-Control

The most interesting, and perhaps the most profound, argument on behalf of sludge insists that far from deploring it, we should celebrate it, as a well-tailored response to human fallibility. In brief: Sludge of diverse kinds might be designed to promote better decisions—to counteract self-control problems, recklessness, and impulsivity. Sludge protects people against their own errors. For that reason, sludge can easily be judged as a sensible cure for a behavioral problem.

Behavioral scientists sometimes contrast two families of cognitive operations in the human mind: System 1, which is rapid, intuitive, and emotional, and System 2, which is deliberative and reflective.[9] Sludge can be a way to strengthen the hand of System 2. When System 1 is agitated, passionate, or on fire, sludge is a kind of yellow light, allowing System 2 to take control.

Consider the case of mundane decisions, for which small amounts of sludge are frequently imposed online. As we have seen, it is standard for people to be asked whether they are sure they want to send an email with nasty language or without a subject line; make a payment; cancel a recent order; change a payment method or address; or delete a file. Such burdens can be an excellent idea. People might be acting impulsively; they might not be paying enough attention. Significant sludge, imposed by private and public institutions, might also make sense for life-altering decisions, such as marriage and divorce.[10] If people are deciding whether to end a marriage, "cooling-off periods" can be a blessing.[11] When emotions are leading people to make rash decisions, a mandatory waiting time might be useful as a way of slowing things down and making sure a momentary impulse is not at work.

Some sludge also makes sense before the purchase of guns, partly as a way of promoting deliberation.[12] In fact, evidence suggests that waiting period laws, imposing sludge and delaying the purchase of firearms by a few days, reduce gun homicides by roughly 17 percent.[13] The seventeen states (including the District of Columbia) with waiting periods eliminate about 750 gun homicides per year as a result of that policy. Expanding the waiting period policy to all other US states would prevent an additional 910 gun homicides per year without restricting who can own a gun. For preventing gun violence, creative uses of sludge could do a great deal of good. In the context of abortion, we have seen that some people defend sludge as a way of increasing reflection and deliberation.

Privacy

Sometimes private and public institutions ask for a lot of personal information. Many people think that if they are to receive that information, it must be with people's explicit consent. A pervasive question is whether to ask people to face time-consuming administrative burdens or instead to intrude on their privacy. Perhaps it is not so terrible if the government, at least, chooses the former.

At one period, of course, officials had no real option. Even if they wanted to intrude on privacy, they could not do so because they lacked the means. Increasingly, however, public institutions (and private ones as well) have independent access to that information, or they might be able to obtain it with a little effort. As a result, they are in a position to reduce sludge. Return, as a simple example, to the direct certification program of the US Department of Agriculture.[14] Officials know who is poor, and so they can directly certify people as such.

In countless other cases, available data can enable private or public institutions to announce, very simply, that certain people are eligible and on what terms. They might know who lived where, who owes what, who committed what crimes, who traveled where, who spoke with whom and when. They might be able to pre-populate forms. Government agencies might be able to share data with one another.[15] Facebook, Google, Twitter, Instagram, YouTube, and the US government could share data. To that extent, sludge can be a thing of the past.

But would that be desirable? To put it gently: not necessarily. In many cases, there is a trade-off between irritating burdens on the one hand and potential invasions of privacy on the other. Consider, for example, the question of how much information credit card companies should acquire, and should be allowed to acquire, before offering cards to customers. We might welcome situations in which such companies can find what they need and simply send eligible people offers or even cards. Or maybe we would not welcome that at all. Whether we should do so depends in part on what information they have and whether it might be misused.

The stakes are probably higher if government has or acquires the relevant information. In the worst cases, we might fear that public officials will use that information to punish their enemies. In harder but still troubling cases, we might fear that public officials will use that information for purposes that have little or nothing to do with the reasons for which it was originally acquired. Within the US government, there is a category called *personally identifiable information* (PII), and the law imposes severe restrictions on its acquisition and use. The very existence of the category suggests that for government, the risks of information acquisition might be thought unacceptable—and hence we might tolerate some sludge. Consider in this light the option of automatic enrollment, which eliminates sludge. That option might well be possible only if we authorize, and are able to get comfortable with, a great deal of information-gathering by institutions that people might not trust.

In recent years, the question of acquisition of information by private companies has become sharply debated. Many people think that the risk of abuse is greatest with government. But with mounting concerns about "surveillance capitalism,"[16] that might not be obvious. Perhaps social media companies, or other big tech companies, can use what they know about each of us to manipulate us to make choices that are in their economic interest. Perhaps they can treat us as puppets on a string. If so, we might want to limit their ability to acquire information and also their ability to use what they get. Concerns of this kind go far beyond the topic of sludge. But if the best way to reduce sludge is to let private institutions acquire personal information on their own, we might think, well, sludge isn't *so* bad.

Security

The question of security is closely related. Sometimes institutions ask for sludge not to annoy anyone, but to make sure that information receives the protection it deserves. To set up an online account, for example, people might be asked to provide, and might be willing to provide, sensitive information. It might involve their bank account or their credit card. People might be asked to answer questions about their address, their Social Security number, or their mother's maiden name. Sludge might be designed to ensure against security violations. Answering these questions is not exactly fun, but they might be justified as a means of ensuring against some kind of breach. Compare two-factor authentication, which imposes sludge. (And just speaking for myself, it is really, really annoying.)

Ideally, of course, we would have some clarity about the benefits and costs of sludge that is designed to protect people's security (a point to which I will return). But if costs and benefits are difficult to specify, it might make sense to have a rough-and-ready sense that a degree of not especially onerous sludge is desirable to prevent the worst-case scenarios.

Targeting

Might sludge be a way of targeting? Might it be a way of ensuring that goods go to the people who most deserve or need them? Might it turn out to be an effective and even fair strategy, the best available option in many settings?

A growing literature on hassles and ordeals explores that possibility. It shows that sludge might operate as a *rationing device*, increasing the likelihood that benefits, including licenses and permits, will be allocated as they ought to be.[17] The intuitive idea is that burdens can improve self-selection. Suppose that a movie or a concert is immensely popular. If so, people might be asked to stay on the telephone or to wait in line for a ridiculously long time. If that approach can be justified, it is because an investment of time, like an expenditure of money, helps measure how intensely people want things. In the same vein, seemingly onerous administrative burdens, and apparently pointless sludge, might be a reasonable way of screening applicants for job training or other programs. If people are really willing to run the gauntlet, we might have good reason to think that they will benefit from those programs.

No one denies the importance of finding good ways to screen those who seek access to scarce resources. In markets, the willingness to pay criterion provides the standard screen; it is meant to ensure that people will receive goods if and only if they are willing to pay for them. If you are willing to pay a certain amount of money for apples or oranges, and no more, we will have a measure of how much you really want apples or oranges. The willingness to pay measure has obvious advantages. It's pretty simple; people use it every day. It's a lot better than randomness. But it also has major problems. Willingness to pay is dependent on ability to pay, and if you are not willing to pay much for apples, or for health care, it might be because you are poor. For many benefits coming from the government, willingness to pay does not make a lot of sense. Would we want to say that people get money to help them cope with a pandemic depending on how much they are willing to pay for it?

Willingness to pay money is just one way to measure people's needs or desires. Another way is willingness to pay in terms of time and effort (WTPT, for short). How much time are you willing to pay to get a driver's license? To get financial aid for education? Because willingness to pay depends on ability to pay, you might think that the willingness to pay criterion discriminates against people without much money. WTPT does not have that particular defect.[18] If anything, *it discriminates against people without much time.* There may or may not be a correlation between lacking money and lacking time.

In any case, government (or the private sector) might choose to use WTPT as a way of targeting—as a way of ensuring that goods are allocated to people who really need and want them.[19]

It is not exactly crazy to think that sludge can be a reasonable way of targeting. Intuitively, that idea makes some sense. The problem is that if the goal really is to target benefits, imposing sludge is often a singularly crude method of doing so. In fact, it can be terrible. A complex, barely comprehensible form for receiving federal aid is not exactly a reliable way to ensure that people who need financial help actually get that help. If public officials want to ensure that people who are eligible for the EITC actually receive it, a degree of sludge is not the best sorting mechanism. Ordeals have their purposes, and sludge can be an ordeal. But it is a hazardous mechanism for targeting.

Actually, it is worse than that. In some cases, ordeals work in concert with the limitations faced by poor people, so as specifically to select out those with the *highest need!*[20]

On reflection, that should not be so surprising. If those with the highest need are also the least likely to wade through sludge—if they suffer from scarcity of multiple kinds—sludge will fail as a targeting mechanism. Suppose that a public institution wants to make mental health services available to those who most need them. Suppose too that sludge is a particular deterrent to those suffering from depression or anxiety. If so, sludge will filter out exactly those people who most need the services. The same problem can be found if sludge is designed to ensure that scarce resources go to the neediest among the poor. It may be that the neediest are in the worst position to navigate sludge.

The problem is pervasive. It highlights a central point here. Sludge should be assessed for its distributional effects. If it has especially adverse consequences for the most disadvantaged members of society, it should be reduced or eliminated.

Acquiring Useful Data

To run a government, public officials need a great deal of information. Among other things, they need to know how programs are working. Public officials might impose sludge to acquire data that can be used for multiple purposes, and that might benefit the public a great deal.

For example, officials might want to know whether people who receive employment training or some kind of educational funding are actually benefiting. What do they do with that training or that funding? Sludge might be essential to obtain answers to that question. Or suppose that the government is trying to reduce the spread of an infectious disease, to promote highway development, to monitor hazardous waste management, to ensure that pilots are properly certified and that airplanes are properly maintained, or to see how food-safety programs are working.[21] Those who receive information-collection requests might complain of sludge. But the relevant burdens might be justified as a means of ensuring acquisition of important or even indispensable knowledge.

A related point involves record-keeping and ongoing monitoring. Public officials need to obtain information about what is happening on the ground, and that can require sludge. In many countries, public officials gave out an immense amount of money to help individuals and institutions cope with the ongoing COVID-19 pandemic, and also to help researchers of multiple kinds. What was the money used for? Where exactly did it go? It is not easy to get answers to those questions without requiring sludge. For people who are subject to it, the process might be burdensome, but if we want to manage public programs, we might well need to impose that burden.

In some of these cases, of course, sludge might be an effort to ensure program integrity. But I am emphasizing a different point. Even if program integrity is already guaranteed, officials might seek information, and require people to provide it, in order to provide both short-term and long-term benefits. Importantly, that information might be made public and used by private and public sectors alike.[22] In the modern era, acquisition of information might promote public and private accountability. It might save money. It might spur innovation. It might even save lives.

These are important justifications for sludge, and they are easy to overlook. But they should not be taken as a kind of blank check or as an open invitation for officials to impose significant administrative burdens. For any particular burden, a central question is whether the government is *actually acquiring useful information.* If public officials are asking people to file with paper rather than electronically, refusing to reuse information that they already have, declining to prepopulate forms, or requiring quarterly rather than annual reporting, they should face a burden of justification. In all of these cases, they might well run into difficulty in meeting that burden.

In the abstract, it is not possible to say whether sludge is justified as a means of generating useful or important information. Some cases will be easy; any such justification will not be credible. Other cases will also be easy; any such justification is self-evidently convincing. Still other cases will be hard; without investigating the details with care, we cannot know whether such a justification is sufficient. The only point is that the benefit of sludge might be found there.

6
Sludge Audits

My goal in this chapter is to see how we might cut sludge. The emphasis is on government, but the general lesson is broader. As we have seen, hospitals impose a lot of sludge; much of it is required by the government, but not all. In education, there is far too much sludge, and it hurts students, teachers, and parents alike. The non-profit sector could do much better if it eliminated sludge. Relationships between employers and employees could be improved if the former took steps to reduce administrative burdens imposed on the latter. But let's begin with a glance at how, exactly, sludge gets weaponized.

Redemption

Mail-in forms provide people with an opportunity to obtain real money, often in the form of a check, but they require people to overcome inertia.[1] With respect to such forms, I received a personal lesson a number of years ago, when I bought a new cell phone. It was quite expensive, but the package came with a mail-in form, with a pleasant opportunity: if you actually mail it in, you will get $200 in return. What a good deal! But I misplaced the form, and after two hours of searching, I just couldn't find it.

Companies are well aware of that challenge. Across various markets, redemption rates are pretty pathetic. They usually range between 10 percent and 40 percent, which means that a strong majority of customers forget or simply do not bother.[2] Because of the power of inertia, that might not be terribly surprising. What is more striking is the finding that people are *unrealistically optimistic* about the likelihood that they will ever redeem forms. Inertia and unrealistic optimism are a fiendish combination, and a marketing opportunity. A company might sell cell phones, or whatever, at a high price, but add that if you just send in a form, you can get a chunk of your money back. If consumers are unrealistically optimistic and suffer from inertia, that is a smart strategy. Most of the time, companies get to keep the money.

The problem is documented in a study with a memorably precise name: *Everyone Believes in Redemption*.[3] In the relevant study, people thought that there was about an 80 percent chance that they would send in a form and collect some money within the thirty days they were given. The actual redemption rate was 31 percent. It is an overstatement to say that everyone believes in redemption—but most people certainly do.

In the same study, the researchers made three efforts (with different groups of people) to reduce the massive difference between the predicted and actual redemption rates. First, they informed participants, very clearly, that in previous groups with similar people, redemption rates were below one-third. Second, they issued two clear reminders, one soon after purchase and another when the deadline for redemption was close. Third, they reduced sludge, making redemption far simpler by eliminating the requirement that people must print out and sign a certification page.

As it turned out, not one of the three interventions reduced people's optimism! In all conditions, people thought there was about an 80 percent chance that they would mail in the forms. Moreover, and somewhat surprisingly, the first two interventions had no effect on what people actually did. When hearing about the behavior of other groups, people apparently thought, "Well, those are *other* groups. What do they have to do with us?" In other contexts, reminders often work because they focus people's attention and reduce the power of inertia. But in this case, reminders turned out to be useless.

Only one of the interventions was effective: simplification, also known as sludge reduction. That intervention had a strong impact on what people actually did. By making it easier for people to mail in the form and thus cutting sludge, simplification significantly increased people's willingness to act. The redemption rate rose to about 54 percent, which means that the disparity between belief and behavior was cut in half. In short, sludge reduction made all the difference. It dramatically altered people's behavior.

Fun with Numbers

Return to a number that we encountered earlier: 11.4 billion. That is the number of hours of paperwork burdens that the US government imposes on the American people. How can that number be reduced?

In a deeply polarized time, that question should appeal to people who disagree on many political issues. Large-scale political divisions—with respect to climate change, tax rates for the wealthy, and immigration—are generally irrelevant to the question whether to reduce sludge. In the United States, both Democratic and Republican administrations have battled against sludge. To be sure, we have seen that on some issues (such as abortion and voting rights), sludge is contentious. But a great deal can be done to reduce sludge without getting close to political divisions. This point should hold in many nations. In Europe, for example, there is far too much sludge, and much of it has grown by accretion, without anyone in a position of authority ever asking: Aren't we requiring too much?

Auditing

When I worked in the White House, I issued a guidance document, requiring federal agencies to test their paperwork burdens—a kind of case-by-case Sludge Audit. This was at the explicit direction of President Obama. The guidance document read as follows:

> To the extent feasible and appropriate, especially for complex or lengthy forms, agencies shall engage in advance testing of information collections, including Federal forms, in order (1) to ensure that they are not unnecessarily complex, burdensome, or confusing, (2) to obtain the best available information about the likely burdens on members of the public (including small businesses), and (3) to identify ways to reduce burdens and to increase simplification and ease of comprehension.[4]

It would be possible to be far more ambitious. A good way to motivate sludge reduction, in both the public and private sectors, is to conduct regular and *general* Sludge Audits, by which people simply try to measure how much sludge is out there. Governments agencies should be conducting Sludge Audits. So should companies of all kinds, and educational institutions as well.

A mundane example: The US Department of Education might begin by measuring the annual paperwork burden that it imposes on the nation's educational institutions. It might start with its own estimates, testing them for accuracy, and then engage those institutions to see if the estimates need adjustment. The department might offer, for its own assessment and preferably for the public, a disaggregated picture, showing where the numbers are highest and where they are lowest. It might specify the different mandates that produce different burdens, and show the magnitude of those burdens on different institutions and subpopulations (e.g., administrators and students).

A full accounting would take a good deal of work (and feel a bit like sludge to those who have to do it). But comparatively speaking, it is unlikely to take *excessive* work. It could also pay big dividends. For example, there is good evidence that sludge is taking a significant toll on the productivity of research.[5] The National Academy of Sciences has found that inconsistent and duplicative requirements—ranging from conflict of interest forms to reporting mandates—are greatly diminishing the return on federal investments.[6]

In the easiest cases, Sludge Audits would immediately show institutions that the existing level of sludge is too high, and not in anyone's interest. The leadership of the Department of Education might well be shocked to see the sheer volume of what is now being required. (In fact, I predict that it would be.) Some of what is now required is undoubtedly too much, and just seeing it might be enough to motivate change.

Or turn to private sector examples. If it turns out to be difficult for consumers to do what must be done to buy a product—say, a refrigerator or an automobile—a company might simplify the experience. Doing so should attract more customers and produce a wide range of reputational benefits. It is not exactly news that consumers have a far worse experience with businesses when it is difficult to obtain a response to their complaints. Many companies, such as Apple, have innovated creatively in an effort to reduce waiting time and to make it easy to fix products that are not working. We could easily imagine a kind of competition to be a sludge-free company with respect to everything that matters to consumers. The same could be true for employees, investors, and students.

At the opposite pole, companies might know, or learn, that sludge is in their interest, and a Sludge Audit would not create an incentive to reduce it. It might well be good business to make it very easy to start a subscription—and sludgy to stop. Careful testing might show that such a strategy is optimal. A complaint process that involves a degree of sludge might not merely filter out unjustified complaints; it might also save money when complaints are justified. Under imaginable circumstances, sludge is in the competitive interest of firms. If so, the question remains: Is this a kind of behavioral market failure for which a regulatory response is appropriate? The answer will often be "yes."

We have seen that every year, the United States compiles an Information Collection Budget. Covering the entire federal government, and compiled by OIRA, the budget collects agency-by-agency burdens and aggregates them. It should not be difficult for governments all over the world to produce a similar Information Collection Budget, cataloging paperwork burdens. As we have seen, some of those burdens are undoubtedly justified. In addition, the worst forms of sludge might not be paperwork at all (consider time waiting in line). But for governments, an Information Collection Budget is an important start, not least because it is likely to spur sludge-reduction efforts.

Private institutions should be producing similar documents, if only for internal use; and public transparency might also be a good idea. Banks, insurance companies, hospitals, and publishers could save a great deal of money by reducing sludge, and they could improve the experience of countless people who interact with them. It is worth underscoring the case of hospitals, in which sludge can not only create immense frustration but also impair health and even cost lives.

The Office of Information and Regulatory Affairs

I have noted that Office of Information and Regulatory Affairs was created by the Paperwork Reduction Act, which it is entrusted with overseeing. As I saw close-up, OIRA has a lot of room to maneuver. One of its jobs is to pass on each and every information-collection request from federal agencies. (The word *request* is a euphemism. Most of the time, the government orders people to produce information.) If the Department of Health and

Human Services wants to collect information from hospitals, or if the Department of Transportation wants to get information from automobile companies, OIRA has the final say. Under the law, it is entitled to say "no" a lot. It could develop a working presumption: no more sludge.

Of course, OIRA is just one part of the federal government, and fights are not much fun. At least some of the time, the officials who work there are tempted to take the path of least resistance and to say "okay" to officials at the Environmental Protection Agency, the Department of Treasury, or the Food and Drug Administration. A great deal depends on the guidance from leadership: Does the OIRA administrator care about excessive paperwork? Is that a priority? But in any particular period, OIRA can do a lot or a little to reduce sludge.

It can mount a war on paperwork burdens. Alternatively, it can ignore them. It can be relatively lenient to agencies when they ask its approval to make information-collection requests—or not. Its leadership can give a strong signal of leniency—or not. Because OIRA assesses such requests on an individual basis, it can work in an ad hoc manner to reduce the volume of paperwork burdens added each year.[7]

More ambitiously, OIRA can work in a more systematic way. Every six months or so, OIRA announces a *data call*, by which it tells federal agencies what it wants them to do with respect to paperwork. With that data call, it can direct agencies to undertake aggressive sludge-reduction efforts.[8] It can also issue binding guidance documents, which might include ambitious targets for burden reduction.[9] It can work with other White House offices, and the president personally, to produce presidential memoranda or executive orders. If the president of the United States orders a reduction in paperwork burdens or directs federal agencies to reduce sludge, we would almost certainly see real movement. (A question: How many times has that happened in American history? Answer: Never.)

Over the last decades, OIRA has not done nearly enough, but it has done some of these things. When I was administrator of OIRA in 2012, for example, the office directed agencies to take specific steps to reduce paperwork burdens.[10] It called for "significant quantified reductions" in burdens, targeting agencies that imposed high paperwork burdens (including the Department of Treasury, the Department of Health and Human Services, the Securities and Exchange Commission, the Department of Transportation, the Environmental Protection Agency, the Department of Homeland Security, the Department of Labor, and the Department of Agriculture). These agencies were instructed to identify at least one initiative that would eliminate two million hours or more in annual paperwork burdens. All agencies were instructed to attempt to eliminate at least fifty thousand hours in annual burdens.[11]

OIRA has repeatedly encouraged the reduction of sludge by directing agencies to use short-form options, allow electronic communication, promote prepopulation of forms, make less frequent information collections, and reuse information that the government already has.[12] These are standard formulations, and they can be enforced with different levels of enthusiasm. The United States and other countries should consider Australia's SmartForms initiative, which uses prepopulation, appears to improve accuracy, and is a terrific sludge reducer.[13]

It is also worthwhile to consider novel formulations, which could be far more aggressive. If we keep the 11.4-billion-hour figure in mind, we might be able to agree that OIRA should undertake an unprecedently bold effort to reduce sludge, with an emphasis on both the flow of new burdens and the existing stock. For purposes of illustration: With a presidential directive (the most powerful instrument) or a directive from OIRA itself (also good), it could announce an initiative that would require, in the next six months, the following:

- Identification of at least three steps to cut existing burdens
- A reduction of existing burdens by least one hundred thousand hours by all agencies that impose significant burdens (by some standardized definition), and a reduction of at least five million hours by the agencies that currently impose the greatest burdens[14]
- A focus on reducing burdens imposed on vulnerable subpopulations, including the elderly, the sick, the disabled, and the poor

• A focus on reducing burdens in cases in which those burdens compromise specified policy priorities of special interest to the current administration, such as education, health care, and transportation

An initiative of this kind could be specified in many different ways. Discussions between OIRA and relevant agencies could undoubtedly produce fresh ideas. With respect to policy priorities, different administrations would make different choices. Some administrations might want to reduce information-collection burdens under the Affordable Care Act; others might emphasize sludge imposed on small businesses and start-ups; others might emphasize burdens imposed on the transportation sector or on educational institutions; others might do all of these. In the domain of education, a great deal should be done to reduce sludge, which imposes a large toll on schools at all levels (and students as well).

Importantly, many administrative burdens are imposed by state and local governments. Although OIRA has no direct authority over them, it should use its convening power to remove sludge, especially where federal, state, and local governments must coordinate.[15]

Courts

There are lurking questions in the background. If the federal government imposes paperwork burdens in violation of the Paperwork Reduction Act, is there a legal remedy? Are courts available? Is sludge unlawful? Ever? Suppose, for example, that the Department of Health and Human Services requires hospitals to fill out a host of confusing or difficult forms. Suppose, too, that the burden is plainly ridiculous and thus inconsistent with the PRA, in the sense that it has not been minimized and has little practical utility. Can hospitals invoke the PRA and seek invalidation of the requirement? The answer is clear: No.

The general rule is that so long as OIRA has approved an information-collection request, people have to comply with it.[16] The clear language of the law suggests that the PRA requires only that an information collection has and displays a control number, which shows that it has been approved by OIRA. That is most unfortunate. Sooner rather than later, the PRA should be amended to allow people to object more broadly. The Administrative Procedure Act—the legal charter for the regulatory state—generally allows judicial review of arbitrary or capricious decisions by public officials.[17] That standard should be applied to sludge as well, given its high cost and intrusiveness. In less technical language: if the government has imposed a paperwork burden or some other kind of sludge, and if that imposition cannot be justified by reference to legitimate reasons for sludge (see chapter 5), courts should be directed to strike it down.

Congress

Should the PRA be amended in other ways? OIRA itself historically has been skeptical of the idea, on the ground that even if one or another amendment would be a good idea, putting the statute in play in Congress would open the door for other amendments, which might turn out to be uninformed or counterproductive. Nonetheless, some ambitious proposals deserve serious consideration. In particular, four reforms would do a great deal to improve the current situation.

1. Much sludge is explicitly mandated by Congress itself. For that reason, the executive branch has no authority to eliminate it under the PRA. That is a serious problem, and it has stymied some good-faith efforts by OIRA and others to eliminate paperwork requirements. Relevant committees of Congress should initiate a process to revisit those requirements and other kinds of sludge, with the goal of reducing them significantly.

2. Congress should require federal agencies to undertake a periodic lookback at existing paperwork burdens—and thus require both general and specific Sludge Audits. The goals would be to see if the current stock of sludge can be justified and to eliminate administrative burdens that are outmoded, pointless, or too costly. This reform would build on existing lookback requirements for regulation in general.[18]

With respect to sludge, the lookback could occur every two years, alongside a requirement of a publicly available report to Congress. That report could be combined with the currently required Information Collection Budget. Ideally, the requirement of Sludge Audits would lead to guidance documents from OIRA, including some sort of template for capturing best practices.

3. Congress should explicitly require agencies to choose the least burdensome method for achieving their goals. This is essentially a requirement of cost-effectiveness, and its importance cannot easily be overstated. If, for example, annual reporting would be as effective as quarterly reporting, then agencies should choose annual reporting. If electronic reporting would be as good as paper reporting, then agencies should allow electronic reporting. As we have seen, current law can be understood to require cost-effectiveness, but an explicit legislative signal would do considerable good. It would put the federal agencies on notice.

4. Congress should explicitly require the benefits of sludge to justify the costs. With respect to paperwork, cost-benefit balancing can be seen as required by the PRA in its current form. But the statute is hardly clear on that point, and my own experience suggests that at OIRA, there is no general sense that agencies must demonstrate that the benefits of paperwork exceed the costs. Here again, Congress should give an explicit signal to this effect.

With respect to sludge, as with regulation in general, it is important to appreciate the difference between cost-effectiveness and cost-benefit analysis. The former requires the least costly way of achieving a specified goal. For that reason, cost-effectiveness is a significant but modest idea, and it should not be contentious. Who would support an unnecessarily costly way of achieving a particular goal?[19] A burden might be cost-effective but nonetheless fail cost-benefit analysis—and therefore be a bad idea. In general, it is important to say that even if a burden is cost-effective, it should also be assessed in cost-benefit terms to ensure that it is worthwhile on balance.

It is true and important that cost-benefit balancing is not always simple for paperwork burdens. When agencies engage in such balancing, the general goal is to compare the social benefits and the social costs, understood in economic terms. A paperwork burden may or may not generate *social* benefits, understood in those terms. When the IRS imposes paperwork burdens on taxpayers, it might be trying to ensure that they do what the law requires. We can speak of economic costs (in terms, perhaps, of monetized hours) and of economic benefits (in terms, perhaps, of dollars gained by the Treasury).[20] But that is not standard cost-benefit analysis. Or sludge might be imposed to ensure that people applying for benefits actually deserve those benefits—as, for example, when the effort is to avoid giving educational subsidies to people who are not entitled to them. Again, that is not standard cost-benefit analysis.

In such cases, a reasonable approach would be to understand the cost-benefit justification not as an effort to compare social costs and social benefits, understood in economic terms, but instead as entailing an assessment of *proportionality*. Are significant costs likely to serve significant legitimate purposes? What is the magnitude of the costs? How big is the burden? What is the magnitude of the gains? Real numbers would help inform decisions and combat excessive burdens. And for reasons previously outlined, the analysis of costs and benefits should include an analysis of distributional effects: Who is being helped and who is being hurt? Is sludge principally affecting (for example) people who are poor, elderly, or sick?

It is worth emphasizing the fact that even a crude form of cost-benefit analysis would be *information forcing*. It would create a stronger incentive for agencies to offer accurate accounts of the number of burden hours and also to turn them into monetary equivalents. It would simultaneously create an incentive for agencies to be more specific, and more quantitative, about the expected benefits of information collections.

We need far more information about the benefits of collecting information. In that regard, a requirement of cost-benefit balancing would be a big help. It should also help to spur improved and perhaps creative ways to test whether the benefits of sludge justify the costs.

7
The Most Precious Commodity

People dedicated to consumer protection, economic growth, workers' rights, environmental protection, sex equality, voting rights, poverty reduction, mental health, immigrants' rights, visa reform, racial justice, and small businesses and start-ups do not march under colorful banners containing the words, "Sludge Reduction Now!" But in light of their own goals, they might want to start doing exactly that.

Sludge infringes on human dignity. It makes people feel that their time does not matter. In extreme cases, it makes people feel that their lives do not matter. True, it is a stretch to see sludge reduction as a complement to the Universal Declaration of Human Rights—but it is not all that much of a stretch.

Sludge works as a penalty; it makes everything worse. For both rational actors and those who display behavioral biases (such as inertia and present bias), sludge frustrates enjoyment of constitutional rights and prevents access to important benefits. Sludge imposes a kind of tax. If governments require 11.4 billion hours of paperwork annually, they are imposing a cost equivalent to about $308 billion. Any such monetary figure greatly understates the actual impact of sludge, economic and psychological. Sludge compromises the most fundamental rights; it can also cost lives.

All over the world, nations should be making an aggressive, across-the-board attack on sludge—for jobs, for education, for voting, for licenses, for permits, for health. Such an effort would call for reductions at the level of program design, including radical simplification of existing requirements and (even better) use of default options to cut learning and compliance costs. Automatic enrollment can drive sludge down to zero and have very large effects for that reason. Where automatic enrollment is not possible or desirable, officials might use an assortment of tools: simplification and plain language; frequent reminders; online, telephone, or in-person help; and welcoming messages to reduce psychological costs.

Both public and private institutions need *Sludge Audits*—an evidence-based approach to sludge, including an effort to weigh its benefits against its costs and a careful assessment of its distributional effects. Is sludge really helping to reduce fraud? By how much? Under permit programs, how many people are refused? Under benefit programs, what are the take-up rates? How do they vary across populations, including the most vulnerable? Are there harmful effects on the elderly, people with disabilities, women, and people of color? What are the compliance costs, in terms of time and money?

To be sure, the answers to these questions will not always be self-evident. If sludge discourages exercise of the abortion right, people will disagree about whether that is a benefit or a cost. If sludge reduces access to a program designed to help the unemployed, some people will be outraged, and other people will think it is fine or even good; perhaps the sludge is designed to improve targeting or to ensure appropriate work incentives. To know whether sludge causes losses or gains, we will sometimes run into intense disagreements about values. But in many cases, such disagreements are uninteresting and irrelevant, and once we investigate the problem, we will see that sludge is not worth the candle.

Recall the war on sludge in 2020 in connection with the coronavirus pandemic. Almost everyone approved of that war. It saved a lot of lives. With respect to sludge, we may not need a war, but we need plenty of battles. In the future, removal of sludge should be a high priority, and for one simple reason: sludge does far more harm than good.

Time is the most precious commodity that human beings have. Let's find ways to give them more of it.

Acknowledgments

As I have noted, my interest in this topic grows largely out of my experience as administrator of the White House Office of Information and Regulatory Affairs (OIRA) under President Barack Obama. I am immensely grateful to my colleagues at the time, and above all to the extraordinary staff of OIRA, for teaching me so much about paperwork burdens and information collections and about what might be done in response.

I have been working with Richard Thaler, a great friend and coauthor, for many years, and he has been instrumental in exploring the problem of sludge. Few things in life are certain, but it is certain that this book would not exist without him. Special thanks too to Cait Lamberton, who first used the term, both for her originality and for valuable discussions. Conversations with Lucia Reisch and Dilip Sloman have been extremely helpful.

I have also been much influenced by three wonderful books that overlap with this one. Scarcity (2016), by Sendhil Mullainathan and Eldar Shafir, focuses brilliantly on the problem of cognitive scarcity, or limited bandwidth, and applies the problem to paperwork and other burdens. Administrative Burden (2019), by Pamela Herd and Donald Moynihan, is an extraordinarily valuable exploration of the effects of such burdens on the operations of government in particular. Life Admin (2019), by Elizabeth Emens, is a lively, wide-ranging, and immensely instructive discussion of many of the tedious tasks of modern life and of the inefficiencies and unfairnesses for which they are responsible. I know that I have not seen further than others, but this little book certainly stands on the shoulders of giants.

Four anonymous reviewers provided valuable comments that greatly improved the manuscript. Emily Taber was, and is, a tremendous editor, and her keen eye made this book much better than it would otherwise be. Thanks to Harvard Law School, and in particular the Program on Behavioral Economics and Public Policy, for valuable support. Lia Cattaneo, Dinis Cheian, Christopher Cruz, Eli Nachmany, and Lukas Roth provided superb research assistance. Sarah Chalfant, my agent, provided indispensable guidance on the project. Kathleen Caruso shepherded the book to completion, minimizing sludge in the process, and Melinda Rankin did a terrific copyedit.

I have drawn here on two essays: *Sludge and Ordeals*, 68 Duke L.J. 1843 (2019); and *Sludge Audits*, Behav. Pub. Pol'y (2020). I am grateful to both journals for permission to do that here.

Notes

1 A Curse

1. The term itself was first used in this general way by Cait Lamberton, first on Twitter and then in Cait Lamberton & Benjamin Castleman, *Nudging in a Sludge-Filled World*, HuffPost (Sept. 30, 2016, 5:41 PM, updated Dec. 6, 2017), https://www.huffpost.com/entry/nudging-in-a-sludgefilled_b_12087688. The authors also called for *Sludge Audits*, though with a somewhat different understanding of that term. Richard Thaler has run with the idea, very productively. See Richard Thaler, *Nudge, Not Sludge*, 361 Science 431 (2018).

2. *City Offers Automatic Admission to Graduating Seniors*, City of W. Sacramento (June 8, 2020, 5:46 PM), https://www.cityofwestsacramento.org/Home/Components/News/News/1734/67.

3. See Elizabeth Emens, Life Admin: How I Learned to Do Less, Do Better, and Live More (2019).

4. Wittgenstein's discussion of language games and family resemblance is sufficient and decisive for these purposes. See Ludwig Wittgenstein, Philosophical Investigations (1953).

5. See generally Matthew Adler, Measuring Social Welfare: An Introduction (2019).

6. See Michael Luca et al., *Handgun Waiting Periods Reduce Gun Deaths*, 114 Proc. Nat'l Acads. Sci. 12162 (2017).

7. *SNAP—Adjusting Interview Requirements Due to Novel Coronavirus (COVID-19)—Blanket Approval*, US Dep't of Agric. Food & Nutrition Serv. (June 3, 2020), https://www.fns.usda.gov/snap/adjusting-interview -requirements-covid-19-blanket-waiver.

8. Press Release, Ctrs. for Medicare & Medicaid Servs., *Trump Administration Makes Sweeping Regulatory Changes to Help U.S. Healthcare System Address COVID-19 Patient Surge* (Mar. 30, 2020), https://www .cms.gov/newsroom/press-releases/trump-administration-makes -sweeping-regulatory-changes-help-us-healthcare-system-address -covid-19.

9. Press Release, FDA, *Coronavirus (COVID-19) Update: FDA Gives Flexibility to New York State Department of Health, FDA Issues Emergency Use Authorization Diagnostic* (Mar. 13, 2020), https://www.fda.gov/news -events/press-announcements/coronavirus-covid-19-update-fda-gives -flexibility-new-york-state-department-health-fda-issues.

10. See Julian Christensen et al., *Human Capital and Administrative Burden: The Role of Cognitive Resources in Citizen-State Interactions*, 80 Public Admin. Rev. 127 (2019), https://onlinelibrary.wiley.com/doi /pdf/10.1111/puar.13134.

11. See Jon Elster, Sour Grapes (1983).

12. In the United States, the federal government does not have a standard number; but in Regulatory Impact Analyses, it has used numbers from the Bureau of Labor Statistics, which reports an average in the vicinity of twenty-seven dollars. See, for example, FDA, FDA-2016-N-2527, Tobacco Product Standard for N-Nitrosonornicotine Level in Finished Smokeless Tobacco Products (Preliminary Regulatory Impact Analysis) 78 (Jan. 2017), https://www.fda.gov/downloads/abo utfda/reportsmanualsforms/reports/economicanalyses/ucm537872 .pdf (https://perma.cc/46HT-25RZ) ("Labor hours are valued at the current market wage as reported by the May 2015 Occupational Employment Statistics published by the Bureau of Labor Statistics (U.S. Bureau of Labor Statistics, 2015)."); *Average Hourly and Weekly Earnings of All Employees on Private Nonfarm Payrolls by Industry Sector, Seasonally Adjusted*, Bureau of Labor Statistics, https://www.bls.gov

/news.release/empsit.t19.htm (https://perma.cc/42WN-8CDG) (listing the average hourly wage across private industries in January 2019 as $27.56).

13. See U.S. Dep't of Agric. Food & Nutrition Serv., Direct Certification in the National School Lunch Program Report to Congress: State Implementation Progress, School Year 2014-2015 2 (2016) ("Direct certification typically involves matching SNAP, TANF, and FDPIR records against student enrollment lists, at either the State or the LEA level.").

14. Id. at 15, 24.

15. See Susan Dynarski & Mark Wiederspan, Student Aid Simplification: Looking Back and Looking Ahead 19 (NBER, Working Paper No. 17834, 2012), https://www.nber.org/papers/w17834; Eric Bettinger et al., The Role of Simplification and Information in College Decisions: Results from the H&R Block FAFSA Experiment 23 (NBER, Working Paper No. 15361, 2009), https://www.nber.org/papers/w15361. For a private sector initiative designed to simplify the process dramatically, see mos.com.

16. See *Automatic Voter Registration*, Brennan Ctr. for Justice (Nov. 7, 2018), https://www.brennancenter.org/analysis/automatic-voter-registration (https://perma.cc/6EPA-GD5T). As of 2018, thirteen states and the District of Columbia have approved automatic voter-registration policies. These states are Alaska, California, Colorado, Georgia, Illinois, Maryland, Massachusetts, New Jersey, Oregon, Rhode Island, Vermont, Washington, and West Virginia. See *History of AVR & Implementation Dates*, Brennan Ctr. for Justice (Nov. 7, 2018), https://www.brennancenter.org/analysis/history-avr-implementation-dates (https://perma.cc/VXY8-RKQB).

17. Rob Griffin, Paul Gronke, Tova Wang & Liz Kennedy, Ctr. for Am. Progress, Who Votes With Automatic Voter Registration? Impact Analysis of Oregon's First-in-the-Nation Program (2017), https://www.americanprogress.org/issues/democracy/reports/2017/06/07/433677/votes-automatic-voter-registration/#fn-433677-2 (https://perma.cc/9L7K-YPWX).

18. For valuable discussion, see generally Elizabeth F. Emens, *Admin*, 103 Geo. L.J. 1409 (2015). In the healthcare context, see George Loewenstein et al., *A Behavioral Blueprint for Improving Health Care Policy*, 3 Behav. Sci. & Pol'y 53, 53–66 (2017).

19. 44 U.S.C. §§ 3501–3521.

20. 44 U.S.C. § 3504(c); emphasis added.

21. For efforts to deregulate in this way, see Memorandum from Cass R. Sunstein, Admin., OIRA, to the Heads of Executive Departments and Agencies (June 22, 2012), https://www.transportation.gov/sites /dot.gov/files/docs/OMB%20Memo%20on%20Reducing%20Report-ing%20and%20Paperwork%20Burdens.pdf (providing direction to agencies consistent with the PRA and Executive Order 13610, Identifying and Reducing Regulatory Burdens); Memorandum from Cass R. Sunstein, Admin., OIRA, to the Heads of Executive Departments and Agencies, and of the Independent Regulatory Commissions (Aug. 9, 2012), https://obamawhitehouse.archives.gov/sites/default/files/omb /inforeg/memos/testing-and-simplifying-federal-forms.pdf.

22. 44 U.S.C. § 3514(a). Notably, there was imperfect compliance with that requirement from 2016 to 2020, with only one such report.

23. OIRA, Information Collection Budget of the United States Government (2017), https://www.whitehouse.gov/wp-content/uploads/2020 /02/icb_2017-FINAL-1.pdf.

24. Regrettably, the Information Collection Budget does not make a distinction between voluntary and involuntary information collections. It is clear, however, that the vast majority are involuntary. For a clue: the Department of Treasury, mostly through the Internal Revenue Service, accounts for over half of the total, and compliance with its information collections is not voluntary.

25. The federal government does not have a standard number, but in Regulatory Impact Analyses, it has used numbers from the Bureau of Labor Statistics, which reports an average in the vicinity of twenty-seven dollars. See, for example, FDA, supra note 12.

2 Sludge Hurts

1. Cf. Cox v. New Hampshire, 312 U.S. 569, 575, 576 (1941) (upholding a licensing scheme that regulated only the "time, place and manner" of speech).

2. Cf. Thomas Emerson, *The Doctrine of Prior Restraint*, 20 Law & Contemp. Probs. 648, 670 (1955) (describing prior restraint as a "particular method of control which experience has taught tends to create a potent and unnecessary mechanism of government that can smother free communication").

3. See Felice J. Freyer, *Emergency Rooms Once Offered Little for Drug Users. That's Starting to Change*, Bos. Globe (Dec. 10, 2018), https://www.bostonglobe.com/metro/2018/12/09/emergency-rooms-once-had-little-offer-addicted-people-that-starting-change/guX2LGPqG1UdAf9xUV9rXI/story.html (https://perma.cc/FH6P-C2UF).

4. See id. (describing Massachusetts General Hospital's efforts to increase emergency-room resources for patients addicted to opioids).

5. I draw here on work with Jeremy Faust. See Jeremy Samuel Faust & Cass R. Sunstein, Opinion, *Cut the Federal Bureaucratic Sludge*, Bos. Globe (Oct. 8, 2019, 5:00 AM), https://www.bostonglobe.com/opinion/2019/10/08/cut-federal-bureaucratic-sludge/JsLjUUdmy2WwA6xdQXjoGI/story.html.

6. See David Cutler & Dan Ly, *The (Paper) Work of Medicine: Understanding International Medical Costs*, 25 J. Econ. Persps. 3 (2011).

7. See Pamela Herd & Donald P. Moynihan, Administrative Burden: Policymaking by Other Means 23 (2019); Donald Moynihan et al., *Administrative Burden: Learning, Psychological, and Compliance Costs in Citizen-State Interactions*, 25 J. Pub. Admin. Res. & Theory 43, 45–46 (2014).

8. See Janet Currie, *The Take Up of Social Benefits* 11–12 (Inst. for the Study of Labor in Bonn, Discussion Paper No. 1103, 2004) (examining rates of enrollment in social benefits within the United States and United Kingdom); see generally Katherine Baicker, William J. Congdon & Sendhil Mullainathan, *Health Insurance Coverage and Take-Up: Lessons from Behavioral Economics*, 90 Milbank Q. 107 (2012)

(examining low health-insurance take-up rates from a behavioral-economic perspective); Carole Roan Gresenz, Sarah E. Edgington, Miriam Laugesen, & José J. Escarce, *Take-Up of Public Insurance and Crowd-Out of Private Insurance Under Recent CHIP Expansions to Higher Income Children*, 47 Health Servs. Res. 1999 (2012) (analyzing the effect of expanding CHIP eligibility on health-insurance take-up rates); Saurabh Bhargava & Dayanand Manoli, *Improving Take-Up of Tax Benefits in the United States*, Abdul Latif Jameel Poverty Action Lab (2015), https://www.povertyactionlab.org/evaluation/improving-take-tax-benefits-united-states (https://perma.cc/TPW8-XDHU) (noting that "many people who are eligible for social and economic benefits do not claim those benefits" in the United States).

9. Regulatory Reform Team, *Case Study: Chicago Licensing and Permitting Reform*, Data-Smart City Solutions (Mar. 19, 2015), https://datasmart.ash.harvard.edu/news/article/case-study-chicago-licensing-and-permitting-reform-647 (https://perma.cc/X3YJ-JSLM) (assessing the regulatory landscape of the city of Chicago, and finding, among other things, that "approximately 17% of zoning licenses were not being processed and sent back due to insufficient information").

10. On this theme, see Cass R. Sunstein, On Freedom (2019).

11. An engaging overview is Richard H. Thaler, Misbehaving (2016).

12. See Benjamin Enke et al., *Cognitive Biases: Mistakes or Missing Stakes?* (CESifo, Working Paper No. 8168, 2020), https://www.ifo.de/DocDL/cesifo1_wp8168.pdf?fbclid=IwAR3NcT1bGAYWjDbRPp7ki6Mfq5IQb-XtJQuMg3hLgVcPvLIWhkRJe81hUeA.

13. Brigitte C. Madrian & Dennis F. Shea, *The Power of Suggestion: Inertia in 401(k) Participation and Savings Behavior*, 116 Q.J. Econ. 1149, 1185 (2001) (identifying inertia as a force working against participation in 401(k) plans); see also John Pottow & Omri Ben-Shahar, *On the Stickiness of Default Rules*, 33 Fla. St. U. L. Rev. 651, 651 (2006) ("It is by now recognized that factors beyond drafting costs might also cause parties to stick with an undesirable default rule.").

14. George Akerlof, *Procrastination and Obedience*, 81 Am. Econ. Rev. 1, 1–17 (1991) (examining several "behavioral patholog[ies]," including procrastination).

15. For an especially dramatic illustration, see Peter Bergman, Jessica Lasky-Fink & Todd Rogers, *Simplification and Defaults Affect Adoption and Impact of Technology, but Decision Makers Do Not Realize This* (Harvard Kennedy Sch. Faculty Research Working Paper Series, Working Paper No. RWP17-021, 2018), https://ssrn.com/abstract=3233874 (https://perma.cc/YWN6-BBCJ).

16. See Ted O'Donoghue & Matthew Rabin, *Present Bias: Lessons Learned and To Be Learned*, 105 Am. Econ. Rev. 273, 273–78 (2015).

17. See Sendhil Mullainathan & Eldar Shafir, Scarcity (2015).

18. Susan Parker, *Esther Duflo Explains Why She Believes Randomized Controlled Trials Are So Vital*, Ctr. for Effective Philanthropy: Blog (June 23, 2011), https://cep.org/esther-duflo-explains-why-she-believes-randomized-controlled-trials-are-so-vital/.

19. See Pamela Herd & Donald P. Moynihan, Administrative Burden: Policymaking by Other Means (2019). For helpful related discussion, see Jessica Roberts, *Nudge-Proof: Distributive Justice and the Ethics of Nudging*, 116 Mich. L. Rev. 1045 (2018). The idea has support in the PRA, which requires "particular emphasis on those individuals and entities most adversely affected." 44 U.S.C. § 3504(c)(3) (2012).

20. Karen Arulsamy & Liam Delaney, *The Impact of Automatic Enrolment on the Mental Health Gap in Pension Participation: Evidence from the UK* (Geary Inst., Working Paper No. 202004, 2020), https://ideas.repec.org/p/ucd/wpaper/202004.html.

21. For a series of demonstrations, see Herd & Moynihan, supra note 19, at 30–31.

22. See text accompanying supra note 19 (explaining that a disproportionate amount of everyday administrative burdens falls on women).

3   Sludge As Architecture

1. See generally Richard H. Thaler & Cass R. Sunstein, Nudge 83–105 (2008) (describing choice architecture).

2. Peter Bergman & Todd Rogers, *The Impact of Defaults on Technology Adoption* 5 (Harvard Kennedy Sch. Faculty Research Working

Paper Series, Working Paper No. RWP17-021, 2018), https://scholar
.harvard.edu/files/todd_rogers/files/bergman_and_rogers_the_
impace_of_defaults.pdf (https://perma.cc/N7GF-BCY9).

3. Id.

4. Id.

5. See, for example, Brigitte C. Madrian & Dennis F. Shea, *The Power of Suggestion: Inertia in 401(k) Participation and Savings Behavior*, 116 Q.J. Econ. 1149, 1184 (2001) (summarizing behavioral changes resulting from 401(k) participation and savings behavior as a result of changing default options). For a discussion of the effect of inertia on choice of travel modes, see Alessandro Innocenti, Patrizia Lattarulo & Maria Grazia Pazienza, *Heuristics and Biases in Travel Mode Choice* 20 (LabSi, Working Paper No. 27/2009, 2009), http://www.labsi.org/wp/labsi27 .pdf (https://perma.cc/P23F-42UL).

6. I draw here on joint work with Alister Martin, who hss been a pioneer in this area. See Alister Martin & Cass R. Sunstein, *In the ER? Sign Up to Vote*, Bos. Globe (Jan. 13, 2020), https://www.bostonglobe .com/2020/01/13/opinion/er-sign-up-vote/.

7. Thom File, US Census Bureau, No. P20–577, Who Votes? Congressional Elections and the American Electorate: 1978–2014.

8. *Why Are Millions of Citizens Not Registered to Vote?*, Pew Charitable Trs. (June 21, 2017), https://www.pewtrusts.org/en/research-and -analysis/issue-briefs/2017/06/why-are-millions-of-citizens-not-reg istered-to-vote.

9. James J. Augustine, *The Latest Emergency Department Utilization Numbers Are In*, ACEP Now (Oct. 20, 2019), https://www.acepnow.com /article/the-latest-emergency-department-utilization-numbers-are-in/.

10. Alisha Liggett et al., *Results of a Voter Registration Project at Two Family Medicine Residency Clinics in the Bronx, New York*, 12 Annals Fam. Med. 466 (2014).

11. *MGH Votes!*, Mass. Gen. Hosp. (Sept. 7, 2018), https://www.mass general.org/news/article/mgh-votes.

12. VotER, https://vot-er.org/ (last visited June 15, 2020).

13. National Voter Registration Act of 1993, 52 U.S.C. § 20507(d) (2012). This provision of the National Voter Registration Act, among other purposes, is aimed to "ensure that accurate and current voter registration rolls are maintained." 52 U.S.C. § 20501(b)(4).

14. This is the practice suggested by federal law. See 52 U.S.C. § 20507(c)(1). Thirty-six states do at least this. See Nat'l Assn. of Sec'ys of State, NASS Report: Maintenance of State Voter Registration Lists 5–6 (2017) (Dec. 2017), https://www.nass.org/sites/default/files/reports /nass-report-voter-reg-maintenance-final-dec17.pdf (https://perma.cc /FXJ6-RPXK). See, for example, Iowa Code § 48A.28.3 (2018) (permitting the sending of notice each year); Ga. Code Ann. § 21-2-234(a) (1)–(2) (2018) (notice sent to registrants with whom there has been "no contact" for three years); Pa. Stat. Ann., tit. 25, § 1901(b)(3) (2018) (notice sent to voters who have not voted in five years); Ohio Rev. Code Ann. § 3503.21(B)(2) (2018) (notice sent to those who fail to vote in two consecutive federal elections). Note also that some states trigger notices based on dubious interstate databases. See, for example, Okla. Admin. Code § 230:15-11-19(a)(3) (2018) (notice sent to those who have not voted since the "second previous General Election" and those who fail references to interstate databases); Wis. Stat. Ann. § 6.50(1) (2018) (notice sent to voters who have not voted in four years). See also Jonathan Brater et al., Brennan Center for Justice at the New York University School of Law, Purges: A Growing Threat to the Right to Vote 7–8 (2018) (explaining how the system used by Oklahoma, "Crosscheck," is unreliable and inaccurate).

15. See 52 U.S.C. § 20507(d)(1)(ii).

16. 52 U.S.C. § 20507(d) makes failure to send the return card back one of the two sufficient conditions for removing a registered voter from the rolls on change-of-address grounds. Husted v. A. Philip Randolph Inst., 138 S. Ct. 1833, 1845 (2018) (rejecting the argument that voters throw away return cards so often as to make them "worthless").

17. For relevant discussion, see Petra Persson, *Attention Manipulation and Information Overload*, 2 Behav. Pub. Pol'y 78 (2018); Thomas

Blake, Sarah Moshary, Kane Sweeney & Steven Tadelis, *Price Salience and Product Choice* (NBER, Working Paper No. 25186, 2018), https://www.nber.org/papers/w25186?sy=186 (https://perma.cc/Y54U-9K9S).

18. See Wendy Wagner, Incomprehensible! (2019).

19. Arunesh Mather et al., *Dark Patterns at Scale: Findings from a Crawl of 11K Shopping Websites*, 3 Proc. ACM Hum.-Comput. Interact. 81 (2019), https://arxiv.org/pdf/1907.07032.pdf.

20. See Xavier Gabaix & David Laibson, Shrouded Attributes, Consumer Myopia, and Information Suppression in Competitive Markets, 121 Q.J. Econ. 505 (2006).

4   Sludge in Action

1. See Pamela Herd & Donald P. Moynihan, Administrative Burden: Policymaking by Other Means (2019).

2. See Wendy Wagner, Incomprehensible! (2019), for valuable discussion.

3. Herd & Moynihan, supra note 1, at 215.

4. Id. at 233.

5. Id. at 215.

6. Id. at 219; 225–226.

7. Id. at 227.

8. Id. at 233.

9. Id. at 237.

10. Id.

11. See Katherine Baicker, William J. Congdon & Sendhil Mullainathan, *Health Insurance Coverage and Take-Up: Lessons from Behavioral Economics*, 90 Milbank Q. 107 (2012).

12.   See Ben Sommers et al., US Dep't Health & Hum. Services: Office of the Assistant Secretary for Planning and Evaluation, *ASPE Issue Brief:*

Understanding Participation Rates in Medicaid: Implications for the Affordable Care Act (2012), https://aspe.hhs.gov/basic-report/understanding-par ticipation-rates-medicaid-implications-affordable-care-act. See Baicker, Congdon & Mullainathan, supra note 11.

13. See id.

14. For a general discussion, see Making Work Pay (Bruce Meyer & Douglas Holtz-Eakin eds. 2002).

15. Herd & Moynihan, supra note 1, at 191.

16. Id. at 196.

17. Id. at 194.

18. Id. at 196.

19. Surprisingly, there appears to be no literature on automatic enroll-ment and the EITC. This area deserves sustained study.

20. Herd & Moynihan, supra note 1, at 213.

21. *Policy Basics: The Supplemental Nutrition Assistance Program (SNAP)*, Ctr. on Budget & Policy Priorities (June 25, 2019), https://www.cbpp .org/research/food-assistance/policy-basics-the-supplemental-nutrition -assistance-program-snap.

22. *SNAP Data Tables*, USDA (May 15, 2020), https://www.fns.usda .gov/pd/supplemental-nutrition-assistance-program-snap.

23. *The Positive Effect of SNAP Benefits on Participants and Communities*, Food Research & Action Ctr., https://frac.org/programs/supplemental -nutrition-assistance-program-snap/positive-effect-snap-benefits -participants-communities (last accessed June 15, 2020).

24. Id. Some people are categorically excluded from SNAP benefits, including students and undocumented immigrants.

25. David Ribar, *How to Improve Participation in Social Assistance Pro-grams*, 104 IZA World of Lab., Dec. 2014, at 3.

26. Karen Cunnyngham, USDA, Reaching Those in Need: Estimates of State Supplemental Nutrition Assistance Program Participation

Rates in 2016 1 (2019); Mark Prell et al., USDA, Annual and Monthly SNAP Participation Rates 2 (2015).

27. Janet M. Currie, The Invisible Safety Net 68–70 (2006).

28. Brian Stacy et al., USDA, Using a Policy Index To Capture Trends and Differences in State Administration of USDA's Supplemental Nutrition Assistance Program 15 (2018).

29. Currie, supra note 27, at 68.

30. Id. at 68–69.

31. *SNAP Online: A Review of State Government SNAP Website*, Ctr. on Budget & Policy Priorities (Jan. 27, 2020), https://www.cbpp.org /research/food-assistance/snap-online-a-review-of-state-government -snap-websites.

32. Hiram Lopez-Ladin, AARP Foundation, SNAP Access Barriers Faced by Low Income 50–59 Year Olds 15 (2013).

33. Id. at 5.

34. Tatiana Homonoff & Jason Somerville, *Program Recertification Costs: Evidence from SNAP* (NBER, Working Paper No. 27311, 2020).

35. Id.

36. Id. at 3.

37. Id. at 4.

38. Id. at 5.

39. C. A. Pinard et al., *What Factors Influence Snap Participation? Literature Reflecting Enrollment in Food Assistance Programs from a Social and Behavioral Science Perspective*, 12 J. Hunger & Envt'l Nutrition 151, 157 (2017).

40. *Policy Basics: Temporary Assistance for Needy Families*, Ctr. on Budget & Policy Priorities (Feb. 6, 2020), https://www.cbpp.org/research/family -income-support/temporary-assistance-for-needy-families.

41. Linda Giannarelli, Urban Inst., What Was the TANF Participation Rate in 2016? 1 (2019).

42. Ife Floyd, *Cash Assistance Should Reach Millions More Families*, Ctr. on Budget & Policy Priorities (Mar. 4, 2020), https://www.cbpp .org/research/family-income-support/cash-assistance-should-reach -millions-more-families.

43. Id.

44. Id.

45. States have significant discretion to determine TANF eligibility and the application process. *Policy Basics: Temporary Assistance for Needy Families*, supra note 40, at 3. The District of Columbia, for example, requires an application, an in-person appointment, and may require an applicant to bring documentation of income, assets, DC residency, her social security number, medical examination reports, immigration information, birth certificates, and statements from non-relatives. See *TANF for District Families*, DC Dep't of Human Servs., https://dhs.dc.gov/service/tanf-district-families (last accessed Aug. 18, 2020); *Documents You May Need for Your Interview*, DC Dep't of Human Servs., https://dhs.dc.gov/service/documents-you-may-need-your-interview (last accessed Aug. 18, 2020).

46. Heather Hahn et al., Urban Inst., Work Requirements in Social Safety Net Programs (2017); Pamela A. Holcomb et al., US Dep't of Health & Human Servs., The Application Process for TANF, Food Stamps, Medicaid and SCHIP 3–9 (2003).

47. Holcomb et al., supra note 46, at v.

48. Barak Y. Orbach, *Unwelcome Benefits: Why Welfare Beneficiaries Reject Government Aid*, 24 Law & Ineq. 108, 120–123 (2006).

49. See *Online Services for Key Low-Income Benefit Programs*, Ctr. on Budget & Policy Priorities (July 29, 2016), https://www.cbpp.org /research/online-services-for-key-low-income-benefit-programs.

50. Id.

51. See Jennifer Stuber & Karl Kronebusch, *Stigma and Other Determinants of Participation in TANF and Medicaid*, J. 23 Pol'y Analysis & Mgmt. 509 (2004).

52. Id.

53. Orbach, supra note 48, at 129–130.

54. Id.

55. Sheila R. Yedlewski, Urban Inst., Left Behind or Staying Away? Eligible Parents Who Remain Off TANF 5 (2002).

56. Id.

57. Patient Protection and Affordable Care Act of 2010, Pub. L. No. 111–148, 124 Stat. 119 (codified as amended in scattered sections of 42 U.S.C. § 18001 (2012)).

58. Herd & Moynihan, supra note 1, at 98.

59. Id. at 99.

60. Id. at 118.

61. See Patient Protection and Affordable Care Act; HHS Notice of Benefit and Payment Parameters for 2021; Notice Requirement for Non-Federal Governmental Plans, 85 Fed. Reg. 7088, 7119–7120 (Feb. 6, 2020).

62. *Sabotage Watch: Tracking Efforts to Undermine the ACA*, Ctr. on Budget & Policy Priorities (June 12, 2020), https://www.cbpp.org /sabotage-watch-tracking-efforts-to-undermine-the-aca.

63. See Alex Olgin, *Reductions in Federal Funding for Health Law Navigators Cut Unevenly*, Nat'l Pub. Radio (Oct. 26, 2017, 12:54 PM), https://www.npr.org/sections/health-shots/2017/10/26/559574743 /money-for-health-law-navigators-slashed-except-where-it-s-not.

64. Press Release, *CMS Announcement on ACA Navigator Program and Promotion for Upcoming Open Enrollment*, CMS.gov (Aug. 31, 2017), https://www.cms.gov/newsroom/press-releases/cms-announcement -aca-navigator-program-and-promotion-upcoming-open-enrollment.

65. See Olgin, supra note 63.

66. Amy Goldstein, *Federal Notices about ACA Enrollment Season Get Cut in Number and Messaging*, Wash. Post (Nov. 1, 2017), https:// www.washingtonpost.com/national/health-science/federal-notices

-about-aca-enrollment-season-get-cut-in-number-and-messaging
/2017/11/01/e0eeb872-bf16-11e7-97d9-bdab5a0ab381_story.html.

67. *Status of State Action on the Medicaid Expansion Decision*, Kaiser
Family Found. (May 29, 2020), https://www.kff.org/about-us/.

68. *Medicaid Expansion & What It Means for You*, HealthCare.gov,
https://www.healthcare.gov/medicaid-chip/medicaid-expansion-and
-you/ (last visited June 14, 2020).

69. Selena Simmons-Duffin, *Trump Is Trying Hard to Thwart Obamacare. How's That Going?*, Nat'l Pub. Radio (Oct. 14, 2019, 3:54 PM),
https://www.npr.org/sections/health-shots/2019/10/14/768731628
/trump-is-trying-hard-to-thwart-obamacare-hows-that-going.

70. Ian Hill & Emily Burroughs, Urban Inst., Lessons from Launch-
ing Medicaid Work Requirements in Arkansas 1 (2019).

71. Id. at 6.

72. Id. at 7.

73. Id. at 15.

74. Id. at 17.

75. Social Security Amendments of 1965, Pub. L. 89–97, 79 Stat. 286
(codified as amended in scattered sections at 25, 26, 29 & 42 U.S.C.
(2012)). Medicare is understood in four parts: hospital insurance in
Part A, 42 U.S.C. § 1395c; supplemental medical insurance in Part
B, 42 U.S.C. § 1395j; managed care in Part C, 42 U.S.C. § 1395w-21;
and drug benefits in Part D, 42 U.S.C. § 1395w-101.

76. Herd & Moynihan, supra note 1, at 134–135.

77. Id. at 134.

78. See Saurabh Bhargava et al., *Choose to Lose: Health Plan Choices
From a Menu with Dominated Options*, 132 Q.J. Econ. 1319, 1322 (2017)
(noting that in both experimental and field studies, individuals did
not select the most financially efficient Medicare plans).

79. Herd & Moynihan, supra note 1, at 138.

80. *Why Occupational Licensing Reform Is Needed*, Charles Koch Inst., https://www.charleskochinstitute.org/issue-areas/stopping-corporate -welfare/why-occupational-licensing-reform-is-needed/ (last visited June 9, 2020).

81. Dick M. Carpenter II et al., Inst. for Just., License to Work: A National Study of Burdens from Occupational Licensing (2d ed. 2017), https://ij.org/wp-content/themes/ijorg/images/ltw2/License_ to_Work_2nd_Edition.pdf.

82. See id. at 16.

83. See id.

84. See *Forms*, S.D. Dep't Labor & Reg.: S.D. Cosmetology Comm'n, https://dlr.sd.gov/cosmetology/forms.aspx (last visited June 11, 2020).

85. See US Dep't of Homeland Sec. & US Dep't of Def., C-FF91556, Report on Barriers to Portability of Occupational Licenses Between States, Appendix C (2018), https://download.militaryonesource.mil /12038/MOS/Reports/barriers-to-portability-of-occupational-licenses -between-states.pdf.

86. NAFSA: Ass'n of Int'l Educators, *Economic Value Statistics* (2019), https://www.nafsa.org/policy-and-advocacy/policy-resources/nafsa -international-student-economic-value-tool-v2.

87. Id.

88. Id.

89. Institute of International Education, What International Students Think About U.S. Higher Education 6 (2015).

90. US Immigration & Customs Enf't, SEVIS by the Numbers: Annual Report on International Student Trends 1 (2018).

91. US Dep't of State, *Non-Immigrant Visa Statistics FY 2019 NIV Detail Table*, https://travel.state.gov/content/travel/en/legal/visa-law0/visa-sta tistics/nonimmigrant-visa-statistics.html.

92. Id.

93. Id.

94. Harvard Int'l Office, *Applying for Your Visa*, https://hio.harvard
.edu/applying-your-visa.

95. US Immigration & Customs Enf't, *I-901 SEVIS Fee Frequently
Asked Questions*, https://www.ice.gov/sevis/i901/faq.

96. US Dep't of State, *DS-160: Online Nonimmigrant Visa Application*,
https://travel.state.gov/content/travel/en/us-visas/visa-information
-resources/forms/ds-160-online-nonimmigrant-visa-application.html
(noting that the information on government websites changes over
time, and the text refers to the provisions of 2020).

97. US Dep't of State, *Student Visa*, https://travel.state.gov/content
/travel/en/us-visas/study/student-visa.html.

98. US Embassy Singapore, *Bank and Payment Options/Pay My Visa
Fee*, https://www.ustraveldocs.com/sg/sg-niv-paymentinfo.asp.

99. For example, the picture must be square, the head of the individual in the picture must be between 1 inch and 1⅜ inches from
the chin to the top of the head, the photo must have been taken
within the last six months, and it must have been taken in full-face
view. US Dep't of State, *Photo Requirements*, https://travel.state.gov
/content/travel/en/us-visas/visa-information-resources/photos.html
. See, for example, US Embassy Singapore, *Photo Studios*, https://sg
.usembassy.gov/u-s-citizen-services/passports/photo-requirements
/photo-studios/.

100. US Embassy & Consulates in the United Kingdom, *The Interview*, https://uk.usembassy.gov/visas/tourism-visitor/the-interview/.

101. Id.

102. Id.

103. US Dep't of State, *Administrative Processing Information*, https://
travel.state.gov/content/travel/en/us-visas/visa-information-resources
/administrative-processing-information.html.

104. Anemona Hartocollis, *International Students Face Hurdles under
Trump Administration Policy, NYT* (Aug. 28, 2019), https://www.nytimes
.com/2019/08/28/us/international-students-visa.html.

105. US Dep't of State, *Nonimmigrant Visa Statistics: FY2019 NIV Workload by Visa Category*, https://travel.state.gov/content/travel/en/legal/visa-law0/visa-statistics/nonimmigrant-visa-statistics.html.

106. Planned Parenthood of Se. Pa. v. Casey, 505 U.S. 833, 874 (1992).

107. See Herd & Moynihan, supra note 1, at 90–92; Kate L. Fetrow, Note, *Taking Abortion Rights Seriously: Toward a Holistic Undue Burden Jurisprudence*, 70 Stan. L. Rev. 319 (2018).

108. Herd & Moynihan, supra note 1, at 71.

109. For a valuable account of how things are happening on the grond, see Mara Buchbinder et al., *"Prefacing the Script" as an Ethical Response to State-Mandated Abortion Counseling*, 7 AJOB Empirical Bioethics 48 (2016), https://www.ncbi.nlm.nih.gov/pmc/articles/PMC4999071/.

110. Herd & Moynihan, supra note 1, at 78–79.

111. Id. at 82.

112. Id.

113. See *How the Knights of Columbus Save Lives: 1,000 Ultrasound Machine Donations* (2019), https://www.catholicnewsagency.com/news/how-the-knights-of-columbus-save-lives-1000-ultrasound-machine-donations-65312.

114. Herd & Moynihan, supra note 1, at 47.

115. Id. at 63–64 (noting the correlation between Republican states and voter ID laws and explaining the correlation with party policies).

116. Vann R. Newkirk II, *The Georgia Governor's Race Has Brought Voter Suppression into Full View*, Atlantic (Nov. 6, 2018), https://www.theatlantic.com/politics/archive/2018/11/how-voter-suppression-actually-works/575035/.

117. Jonathan Brater et al., Brennan Center for Justice at the New York University School of Law, Purges: A Growing Threat to the Right to Vote 1 (2018).

118. See Herd & Moynihan, supra note 1, at 53.

119. Ella Nilsen, *Why New York City Voter Rolls Were Missing Names Again, Explained*, Vox (Sept. 13, 2018, 3:30 PM), https://www.vox.com/2018/9/13/17855254/new-york-city-voters-rolls-purges-missing-names-2018-midterms.

120. Brater et al., supra note 117, at 5–6.

121. See *Voter Identification Requirements: Voter ID Laws*, Nat'l Conference of State Legislatures, http://www.ncsl.org/research/elections-and-campaigns/voter-id.aspx (https://perma.cc/QF6Z-VAKK) (noting that thirty-four states have laws requesting or requiring voters to show some form of identification to vote, and seven of those require state-issued photo identification).

122. Denise Lieberman, *Barriers to the Ballot Box: New Restrictions Underscore the Need for Voting Laws Enforcement*, 39 Hum. Rts. 2, 3 (2012).

123. Rebekah Barber, *The Long Fight over Using Student IDs to Vote in North Carolina*, Facing South (Oct. 22, 2019), https://www.facingsouth.org/2019/10/long-fight-over-using-student-ids-vote-north-carolina.

124. See Herd & Moynihan, supra note 1, at 52.

125. Id. at 2.

126. Sendhil Mullainathan, *For Racial Justice, Employees Need Paid Hours Off for Voting*, NYT (June 12, 2020), https://www.nytimes.com/2020/06/12/business/for-racial-justice-employees-need-paid-hours-off-for-voting.html.

5   Reasons for Sludge

1. See 6 U.S.C. § 795 (2012) ("The Administrator shall ensure that all programs within the Agency administering Federal disaster relief assistance develop and maintain proper internal management controls to prevent and detect fraud, waste, and abuse."); Jerry L. Mashaw & Theodore R. Marmor, *Conceptualizing, Estimating, and Reforming Fraud, Waste, and Abuse in Healthcare Spending*, 11 Yale J. on Reg. 455 (1994); Julie K. Taitsman, *Educating Physicians to Prevent Fraud, Waste, and Abuse*, 364 New Eng. J. Med. 102, 102 (2011).

2. For an example, see US Office of Pers. Mgmt., Standard Form 86: Questionnaire for National Security Positions (2010), https://www.opm .gov/forms/pdf_fill/sf86-non508.pdf (https://perma.cc/KB9P-JJ8D).

3. For a prescient discussion, see generally Ekambaram Paleenswaran & Mohan Kumaraswamy, *Recent Advances and Proposed Improvements in Contractor Prequalification Methodologies*, 36 Building & Env't 73 (2001).

4. Note the emphasis on prepopulation in Memorandum from Neomi Rao, Admin., OIRA, to Chief Information Officers 8 (Aug. 6, 2018), https://www.whitehouse.gov/wp-content/uploads/2018/08/Mini mizing-Paperwork-and-Reporting-Burdens-Data-Call-for-the-2018 -ICB.pdf (https://perma.cc/KF9L-N6NZ), hereinafter Memorandum from Neomi Rao (Aug. 6, 2018) ("Sometimes agencies collect data that are unchanged from prior applications; in such circumstances, they may be able to use, or to give people the option to use, pre-populated electronic forms.").

5. See Austan Goolsbee, Brookings Inst., The "Simple Return": Reduc- ing America's Tax Burden through Return-Free Filing 2 (2006), https:// www.brookings.edu/wp-content/uploads/2016/06/200607goolsbee .pdf (https://perma.cc/C695-5YQL) ("For the millions of taxpayers who could use the Simple Return, however, filing a tax return would entail nothing more than checking the numbers, signing the return, and then either sending a check or getting a refund.").

6. See Memorandum from Neomi Rao (Aug. 6, 2018), supra note 4, at 8 ("Also worth considering is whether, in some circumstances, to dispense with forms entirely and to rely on more automatic, generic, or direct approval of participation.").

7. See Protecting Americans from Tax Hikes (PATH) Act, Pub. L. No. 114–113, 129 Stat. 2242 (2015) (referring to Title II as "Program Integ- rity" and specifically intending to reduce fraudulent and improper payments in the EITC and other programs); Leslie Book et al., *Insights from Behavioral Economics Can Improve Administration of the EITC*, 37 Va. Tax Rev. 177, 180 (2018) (noting that "program integrity" of the EITC was an important topic among employees of the IRS because 43 to 50 percent of all EITC returns are incorrect, with most errors benefitting claimants); *Program Integrity*, Ctrs. for Medicare

& Medicaid Servs., https://www.medicaid.gov/medicaid/program
-integrity/index.html (https://perma.cc/2ZMC-XTSH) (Medicaid Program Integrity); *Reducing Improper Payments*, Soc. Sec. Admin., https://
www.ssa.gov/improperpayments (https://perma.cc/T8ZN-XA32) (Social
Security programs).

8. See, for example, Husted v. A. Philip Randolph Inst., 138 S. Ct.
1833, 1848 ("The NVRA plainly reflects Congress's judgment that
the failure to send back the card, coupled with the failure to vote
during the period covering the next two general federal elections, is
significant evidence that the addressee has moved.").

9. See Daniel Kahneman, Thinking, Fast and Slow 13–15 (2011).

10. See, for example, Fla. Stat. Ann. § 741.04 (2018) (making the effective date of marriage licenses three days after application unless both
partners take a premarital education course); Mass. Ann. Laws ch. 208,
§ 21 (LexisNexis 2018) (allowing divorce to become absolute ninety
days after the initial judgment).

11. See Pamaria Rekaiti & Roger Van den Bergh, *Cooling-Off Periods in
the Consumer Laws of the EC Member States: A Comparative Law and Economics Approach*, 23 J. Consumer Pol'y 371, 397 (2000) ("Cooling-off
periods are potential remedies for the problems of irrational behaviour,
situational monopoly, and informational asymmetry."); Dainn Wie
& Hyoungjong Kim, *Between Calm and Passion: The Cooling-Off Period
and Divorce Decisions in Korea*, 21 Feminist Econ. 187, 209 (2015) ("The
cooling-off period has no significant impact on divorce rates when the
cause of divorce is . . . dishonesty, abuse, or discord with other family
members. . . . Couples reporting the cause of divorce as personality difference or financial distress responded to the cooling-off periods.").

12. See, for example, Cal. Penal Code § 26815(a) (2018) (requiring a
waiting period of ten days for all firearm purchases).

13. Michael Luca et al., *Handgun Waiting Periods Reduce Gun Deaths*,
114 Proc. Nat'l Acads. Sci. 12162 (2017).

14. See U.S. Dep't of Agriculture, Direct Certification in the National
School Lunch Program Report to Congress: State Implementation
Progress, School Year 2014-2015 2 (2016) ("Direct certification typically

involves matching SNAP, TANF, and FDPIR records against student enrollment lists, at either the State or the LEA level.").

15. On some of the relevant trade-offs, see generally Memorandum from Jeffrey D. Zients, Dep. Dir. for Mgmt., & Cass R. Sunstein, Admin., OIRA, to the Heads of Executive Departments and Agencies (Nov. 3, 2010), https://obamawhitehouse.archives.gov/sites/default/files/omb/me moranda/2011/m11-02.pdf (https://perma.cc/56QK-7HCR) (encouraging federal agencies to share data to improve program implementation while complying with privacy laws).

16. See Shoshana Zuboff, The Age of Surveillance Capitalism: The Fight for a Human Future at the New Frontier of Power (2019).

17. Examples include Albert Nichols & Richard Zeckhauser, *Targeting Transfers through Restrictions on Recipients*, 72 Am. Econ. Rev. 372 (1982); Vivi Alatas et al., *Ordeal Mechanisms in Targeting: Theory and Evidence from a Field Experiment in Indonesia* (NBER, Working Paper No. 19121, 2013), https://www.nber.org/papers/w19127.pdf (https:// perma.cc/6XFF-QP8E); Amedeo Fossati & Rosella Levaggi, Public Expenditure Determination in a Mixed Market for Health Care (May 4, 2004) (unpublished manuscript), https://papers.ssrn.com/sol3/papers .cfm?abstract_id=539382 (https://perma.cc/GF5A-YRY5); Sarika Gupta, Perils of the Paperwork: The Impact of Information and Application Assistance on Welfare Program Take-Up in India (Nov. 15, 2017) (unpublished Ph.D. job market paper, Harvard University Kennedy School of Government), https://scholar.harvard.edu/files/sarikagupta /files/gupta_jmp_11_1.pdf (https://perma.cc/K4HY-3YK4).

18. Note that if people are willing to pay others to do a relevant task, such as waiting in line or preparing taxes, the difference between WTP and WTPT might be erased.

19. The IRS provides free online tax preparation to 60 percent of taxpayers. IRS' Intent to Enter into an Agreement with Free File Alliance, LLC (i.e., Free File Alliance), 67 Fed. Reg. 67,247 (Nov. 4, 2002). The program is available for free to taxpayers with income less than $66,000 annually. IRS, *About the Free File Program* (Nov. 21, 2018), https://www.irs.gov/e-file-providers/about-the-free-file-program (https://perma.cc/L5CL-X4ZG).

20. See Gupta, supra note 17, at 30–31.

21. Some of these examples are drawn from OIRA's Information Collection Dashboard. *Information Collection Review Dashboard*, OIRA, https:// www.reginfo.gov/public/jsp/PRA/praDashboard.myjsp?agency_cd=0000 &agency_nm=All&reviewType=EX&from_page=index.jsp&sub_index=1 (https://perma.cc/8X7M-9RHE). For those who are interested in sludge reduction or in information collection in general, the dashboard (typically neglected by scholars) is worth careful attention.

22. See Data.gov, where the US government provides a great deal of useful information, much of it emerging from information-collection requests.

6   Sludge Audits

1. See Matthew Edwards, *The Law, Marketing and Behavioral Economics of Consumer Rebates*, 12 Stan. J.L. Bus. & Fin. 362, 419–421 (2007).

2. Id. at 108.

3. Joshua Tasoff & Robert Letzler, *Everyone Believes in Redemption: Nudges and Overoptimism in Costly Task Completion*, 107 J. Econ. Behav. & Org. 107, 115 (2014).

4. Memorandum from Cass R. Sunstein, Admin., OIRA, to Heads of Executive Agencies and Departments, Testing and Simplifying Federal Forms (August 9, 2012), https://obamawhitehouse.archives.gov/sites /default/files/omb/inforeg/memos/testing-and-simplifying-federal -forms.pdf.

5. *Inconsistent, Duplicative Regulations Undercut Productivity of U.S. Research Enterprise; Actions Needed to Streamline and Harmonize Regulations, Reinvigorate Government-University Partnership*, Nat'l Acads. Sci., Eng'g, & Med. (Sept. 22, 2015), https://www8.nationalacademies.org /onpinews/newsitem.aspx?RecordID=21803.

6. Nat'l Acads. of Sci., Eng'g, & Med., Optimizing the Nation's Investment in Academic Research: A New Regulatory Framework for the 21st Century (2016), https://www.nap.edu/catalog/21824/optimizing-the -nations-investment-in-academic-research-a-new-regulatory.

7. OIRA provides a public account of information-collection requests under review. The account deserves far more attention, academic and otherwise, than it has received to date. See Information Collection Review Dashboard, OIRA, https://www.reginfo.gov/public/jsp /PRA/praDashboard.myjsp?agency_cd=0000&agency_nm=All&rev iewType=RV&from_page=index.jsp&sub_index=1 (https://perma.cc/PD 5L-9BNJ).

8. See, for example, Memorandum from Neomi Rao, Admin., OIRA, to Chief Information Officers 8 (Aug. 6, 2018), https://www.whitehouse .gov/wp-content/uploads/2018/08/Minimizing-Paperwork-and -Reporting-Burdens-Data-Call-for-the-2018-ICB.pdf (https://perma.cc /KF9L-N6NZ), hereinafter Memorandum from Neomi Rao (Aug. 6, 2018) (including a request that agencies reduce paperwork burdens in a data call); Memorandum from Cass R. Sunstein, Admin., OIRA, to the Heads of Executive Departments and Agencies (June 22, 2012), https://www .transportation.gov/sites/dot.gov/files/docs/OMB%20Memo%20on%20 Reducing%20Reporting%20and%20Paperwork%20Burdens.pdf, hereinafter Memorandum from Cass R. Sunstein (June 22, 2012) (same).

9. Memorandum from Cass R. Sunstein, Admin., OIRA, to the Heads of Executive Departments & Agencies & Independent Regulatory Agencies (Apr. 7, 2010), https://www.whitehouse.gov/sites/whitehouse.gov/files /omb/assets/inforeg/PRAPrimer_04072010.pdf (https://perma.cc/D3VW -ZD8T).

10. See Memorandum from Cass R. Sunstein (June 22, 2012), supra note 7.

11. Id.

12. Memorandum from Neomi Rao (Aug. 6, 2018), supra note 7; see also Memorandum from Howard Shelanski, Admin., OIRA, and John P. Holdren, Dir., Off. of Sci. & Tech. Pol'y, to the Heads of Executive Departments & Agencies and of the Independent Regulatory Agencies (Sept. 15, 2015), https://obamawhitehouse.archives.gov/sites/default /files/omb/inforeg/memos/2015/behavioral-science-insights-and-fed eral-forms.pdf (https://perma.cc/M8MX-9K6C) (recommending the use of behavioral sciences when crafting initiatives to reduce paperwork-burden hours).

13. *SmartForms*, Australian Gov't, Dep't of Indus., Sci., Energy, & Res. (Feb. 3, 2020), https://www.industry.gov.au/government-to-government /smartforms.

14. See Memorandum from Cass R. Sunstein (June 22, 2012), supra note 7 (recommending a reduction of two million burden hours for those agencies imposing the highest burden and a reduction of fifty thousand burden hours for all other agencies).

15. See Dep't of the Treasury Off. of Econ. Pol'y, Council of Econ. Advisers, Dep't of Labor, Occupational Licensing: A Framework For Policymakers (July 2015), https://obamawhitehouse.archives.gov/sites /default/files/docs/licensing_report_final_nonembargo.pdf (https:// perma.cc/67Z3-26CV) (demonstrating the power of the federal government to convene state and local government officials and recommending elimination of other forms of sludge).

16. See Pac. Nat. Cellular v. United States, 41 Fed. Cl. 20, 29 (1998).

17. 42 U.S.C. § 706.

18. See Cass R. Sunstein, *The Regulatory Lookback*, 94 B.U. L. Rev. 579, 592–596 (2014).

19. It is true, however, that paperwork burdens can be seen as a kind of tax—and for some purposes, a tax should be increased. Consider paperwork burdens imposed on tobacco companies as part of a regime of regulation. It is not obviously unreasonable to think that although cost minimization is generally a good idea, it is not necessarily a good idea if it reduces the equivalent of a tax imposed on harm-creating activity. Perhaps OIRA should not work especially hard to minimize paperwork burdens imposed on cigarette companies. This point is meant not to offer a final conclusion but simply to flag the issue.

20. For relevant discussion, see generally David Weisbach, Daniel J. Hemel, & Jennifer Nou, *The Marginal Revenue Rule in Cost-Benefit Analysis*, 160 Tax Notes 1507 (2018).

.

Index